Clockwise:
Len T. Smith, Leavenworth, 1904. Smith later became a writer for the Leavenworth Times. *Photographer, Harry Putney.*

School girls of Leavenworth, c. 1890. Photographer, Harry Putney.

E. E. Henry (left) with his friend Dr. Elbee and a wet-plate camera, 1884.

Mrs. Cook, Leavenworth, 1905. Photographer, Harry Putney.

Opposite page, top:
Albert Norton, Leavenworth, early 1900s. Photographer, Horace Stevenson.

Bottom:
The "Goose Town Lick Skillet" section of Leavenworth, 1869. Photographer, E.E. Henry.

The WEST

an american experience

compiled and edited by

DAVID R. PHILLIPS

with commentary
by DAVID R. PHILLIPS
and ROBERT A. WEINSTEIN

HENRY REGNERY COMPANY • CHICAGO

Library of Congress Cataloging in Publication Data
Phillips, David R   1931-
    The West: an American experience.
        1. The West—History—Pictorial works.
    I. Title.
    F591.P44   917.8'03'0222   73-6471

Copyright © 1973 by David R. Phillips. All rights reserved.
Published by Henry Regnery Company
114 West Illinois Street, Chicago, Illinois 60610
Manufactured in the United States of America
Library of Congress Catalog Card Number: 73–6471

Clockwise:
The Santa Fe Trail, leading southwest out of Leavenworth, Kansas, 1869. Photographer, E. E. Henry.

The Rouche family, Leavenworth, 1878. Photographer, E. E. Henry.

Stove made by the Western Manufacturing Company, Leavenworth, 1893. Photographer, Horace Stevenson.

Bill Glick, Leavenworth, 1903. Photographer, Harry Putney.

Opposite page, top:
Leavenworth family, 1920. Photographer, Horace Stevenson.

Bottom:
Captain Taylor, Chief of Police, Leavenworth, c. 1900. Photographer, Horace Stevenson.

Front endsheet: *Near San Francisco, early 1900s*

Back endsheet: *Colorado, late 1880s*

Contents

To the memory of the photographers who made this book possible—Mary Everhard, E. E. Henry, Harrison Putney, Richard Stevenson, Horace Stevenson, Silas Melander, Joseph E. Smith, Edward A. Bass, N. A. Forsyth, Seneca Ray Stoddard, Edward Prawitz, and Irwin Rew.

Clockwise:
Ann Charey, Leavenworth, 1896. Photographer, Horace Stevenson.

Leavenworth home, c. 1890. Photographer, Horace Stevenson.

Unknown subject, 1887. Photographer, Harry Putney.

Leavenworth, 1869. Photographer, E.E. Henry.

Opposite page:
Charles Haun and friends, Leavenworth, 1889.

Introduction

In the nineteenth century, after the birth of photography, one could expect that, of all the photographs taken, there must have been many that were extraordinary. But, hitherto, one has seldom come across such pictures. Whatever the reason—often pictures of "ordinary" people and places simply were not important enough to be carefully preserved, though it was that very quality of ordinariness that made the West—we have seldom been able to view the West as it truly was.

In *The West,* some of those pictures have been presented for open, searching examination and understanding and appreciation of the pioneer during a time that is gone from us. Through these photographs we can share the experiences and challenges of the early Westerners. More to the point, they are brilliant photographic images, by any aesthetic standard, timeless documents made by early photographers struggling to make a living on the western frontier, attempting to record a phenomenon that they may not have understood fully.

Given the quality of the photographs reproduced in *The West,* one may well ask why they were hidden so long from public view. Simply: pictures were lost. Ravaging fires destroyed studios by the score. Glass negatives were broken or, much too heavy to transport, were left behind when a photographer moved to a new location. As we have said, many photographs were considered not "worth" preserving. And yet, as *The West* shows, part of that photographic heritage exists, and more may still be discovered somewhere—collecting dust, waiting to be found in an attic, a loft, a basement, a barn, a forgotten treasure of photographs that could have deep and lasting social value.

Tragically often, we are too late. Many times in my own search for early negatives I have had the descendants of the photographer tell me: "You just missed the negatives. We sent box after box to the dump last week (or last month). We couldn't find anyone that wanted them, not even for picture-frame glass. It's good glass, you know."

The situation, of course, is not always so grim. The negatives of Leavenworth, Kansas, photographer Mary Everhard were a different story. When I asked her if she had her negatives intact, she replied, "Yes, all forty thousand of them." In the back room of her studio, on shelves stretching from floor to fourteen-foot ceiling and completely around the room, were negatives of every size and description. Knowing the historic value of these images, Mary Everhard had cared for them through two Kansas tornados, roof leaks, new locations, and, as she put it, "one small flood." Along with her own marvelous work, Miss Everhard's collection consisted of wet-plate negatives of her studio's predecessors, E. E. Henry and his stepson Harrison Putney, and Richard Stevenson and his son Horace Stevenson, all pioneer photographers of Leavenworth. Not only had Mary Everhard saved and moved her negatives carefully from location to location, she had categorized and catalogued wet-plate negatives for some forty years. In her later years, with so many negatives and subject areas to work with, she had resorted to placing her best negatives in cigar boxes marked "The most," "The very most," and, finally—her ultimate classification—"Glory hole."

Miss Everhard and others have had not a few negatives in their glory holes, and the wonder really is not that there are so few but that there are so many. The difficulties of wet-plate photography, not to mention those of preservation, are staggering. In our age of automatic, motorized cameras and ready-to-use sheet and roll film, it is hard to realize the astronomical difficulty of assuring good quality—not to mention actual physical danger—the early photographers endured in order to take their pictures.

Although the physical danger diminished—though it did not disappear—with the development of glass wet-plate techniques, the difficulties inherent in photography were little diminished, as an examination of the new techniques shows. The process stems from the discovery, in 1846—seventeen years after Daguerre announced his discovery to the world—of gun-cotton. Some predicted gun-cotton would replace gunpowder, but it was soon found to be useless as an explosive agent. However, by 1850, gun-cotton was being dissolved in alcohol or ether to produce an albumen-like substance called collodion, named from the Greek word signifying "to stick," and collodion was found to be the perfect substance, mixed in solution with light-sensitive chemicals, to pour over a glass plate for the production of wonderfully photographic negative plate material. There were some imperfections in the process, of course. For example, if the collodion solution was allowed to dry on the plate, it was not sensitive to light and therefore could not be used to take a picture. However, used almost tacky wet, the collodion film would expose the now-sensitive plate at the rate of about ASA 1.

Outside exposures would take from one to fifteen seconds and the negative had to be developed immediately. Making one wet-plate picture was an act demanding profound care, from cleaning the glass, through coating and exposing the negative, to final on-location developing of the image. One speck of dust on the sticky glass negative would ruin the picture. Water for mixing developing solutions and washing the finished plate negative was always a problem. One photographer in the 1870s, taking pictures in the mountains, found no running water at his high elevation. He solved the problem by catching falling snowflakes on a black rubber blanket and letting the warmth of the sun melt enough snow to enable him to mix the necessary developing and fixing solutions. Final washing was deferred till later.

The days of pioneer photography, along with the hardships and often amusing experience of on-location wet-plate negative developing, came to an end, largely, in the late 1880s. Dry-plate negatives, which did not need immediate development, and compact cameras, enlargements, roll films, and Kodaks were on the market. Yet in some forty years great pioneering photographic work had been done by wet-plate photographers, who had both established and developed photographic technology, science, and art.

The early Western photographers are gone from us now, of course, their time long since past. But a rich visual heritage lives through their pictures. *The West,* a collection of some of the best surviving glass wet-plate negatives, is designed to exhibit these great but largely unrecognized artists' work and to offer a new generation a true picture of the American West.

Clockwise:
Unidentified Leavenworth preachers, 1883. Photographer, E.E. Henry.

General Philip Sheridan's Winchester charger, 1869. Photographer, E.E. Henry.

Opposite page:
Wooden sidewalks bordering the entrance road into Fort Leavenworth, 1869. Photographer, E.E. Henry.

Following page:
Dick Pitman's dog, 1875. Note hands holding dog's head. Photographer, E.E. Henry.

DAVID R. PHILLIPS

Foreword

Almost from the beginning of the American experience a group of ordinary and unsung people lived along the outer fringe of settlement. Hunting, farming, bartering their produce, and gradually creating a society that was to be called "the most American part of America," they provided the cutting edge of the westward movement. When they had completed their sweep of the continent, the tiny seed sown along the Atlantic Seaboard had grown into a new nation.

In the early years, as the pioneer families worked their way across the Appalachian range and down into the Ohio and Mississippi Valleys, they perfected what might be termed their "frontiersmanship," achieving a subsistence living and enjoying certain creature comforts taken from the land. But after they crossed the Missouri River and moved out onto the high plains and into the Rockies, the mode of living changed. Out of these conditions came a people today regarded as typically western.

Historians later would seize upon the dramatics of this great development, and their readers would learn much about trappers, miners, colorful cavalry units, gamblers, and shady ladies and about steamboats, prairie schooners, and pioneer railroads. But it was more difficult to portray the mundane lives of the ordinary members of this army of emigrants. Novelists captured some of the stark reality of daily life on the plains, but, in the main, the story of privation and the struggle against nature remained untold. Even the more talented writers could not explain fully the nuisance of perpetually muddy streets, of endless winds that kept nerves taut, or the maddening monotony of life in a twelve-by-twelve tarpaper homesteader's shack. Extremes of heat, of cold, and of distance were less dramatic enemies than were the native tribes; nevertheless, they were enemies, unrelenting, omnipresent.

The saga of the average American who went west, lived his life, and quietly passed on is one of detail, not of major individual accomplishment. When these minuscule bits of human existence are fitted together, a new picture emerges: a story of the little people who were unaware that without any particular heroics they had accomplished a major transformation in American history.

Latter-day Americans would read of the hell-roaring days of a Dodge City or an Abilene, of shootouts in saloons and death at high noon in a dusty main street as cowboy royalty dueled to the death. But few "westerns," either in print or on movie film, told of the merchant, the livery-stable proprietor, the attorney, the schoolmaster, or the impoverished small-town preacher and how each gave years in support of a little prairie community.

Not much notice would be made of the transformation of these little cow towns into agricultural headquarters and what they contributed to the development of the countryside. Not that the violence of life disappeared; there would be tornadoes, epidemics, and other deadly threats. But somehow the idea of dying from diphtheria was not as dramatic as being launched into eternity by Mr. Colt's hand gun. The great enemy, cholera, found little place in the history of western communities, because it did not speak of the violence of man against man.

Nor is there much discussion of the heartbreak of bankruptcy, of the collapse of a small business that failed to survive the rigors of the desert country, or of the farmer burned out by hot winds or eaten up by clouds of grasshoppers. This was slow death, and there was an almost biblical acceptance of it in the minds of the people.

The real index to man's struggle against western elements is found in his face. The crow's feet around the eyes, etched by raw wind; the permanent squint, implanted by a blazing sun; deep furrows ploughed into the brow. All these, dominated by fierce, unyielding eyes that shouted, "No surrender!" shape a miniature portrait of the price exacted by daily life. It is seen also in the women—with their faded ginghams, their leathery complexions, their chapped and toughened hands—all grim revelations of a life of hardship and toil, of sacrifice and hope, of stubborn determination to survive a bitter climate in a new land.

Here, now, is the last of many Wests: the undeveloped geographical expression that became a reality, the barren and difficult barrier to better days. The time portrayed—from the 1850s to the early 1900s—comes alive, glimpses of it caught by the camera lens, whose sharp eye has captured what authors have failed to reproduce. Shown in the pages that follow are its common people: the townsman, the farmer-frontiersman, the miner and cattleman and soldier and Indian. Here is that unique American experience: the West.

ROBERT G. ATHEARN

The
Photographers'
Gallery

E. E. Henry (1826-1917)

Paris, France, August 19, 1839. Louis Daguerre had just publicly announced his astonishing new photographic discovery. His invention, the daguerreotype, was a sheet of copper coated with silver and made chemically sensitive to light. The copper was exposed in a wood camera and developed by vapors of heated mercury. Excited manufacturers went into phenomenal production. Opticians, carpenters, tailors, sheet metal workers, chemists, and plate makers frantically produced thousands of cameras and photographic plates for buyers eager to start taking pictures.

In order to learn about this new process, young Englishman Ebenezer Elijah Henry left his native England for Paris, where he learned to make daguerreotypes. He learned his trade well. In the middle 1850s he opened a studio in Oshawa, Canada. Well into the 1860s he worked as a photographer in Chicago. Next we find Mr. Henry on a steamboat headed for the very edge of the western frontier. He landed at Leavenworth, Kansas, a small "fittin' out" prairie town on the Missouri River, where he established a portrait studio on Delaware Street in 1864.

The whole panorama of western emigration passed before his cameras. Both in his studio and along the mud-paved streets Mr. Henry made stunning pictures of Leavenworth and its people. By that time the wet-plate negative process was used in the camera for film. E. E. Henry mastered the use of the wet-plate glass negative and thoughtfully took extra caution to preserve his wet plates for the future. His pictures of Leavenworth are considered the finest examples of an early western town.

Henry took great pride in telling a story about a photographic assignment he had taken at nearby Fort Leavenworth. Pictures of one of General Philip Sheridan's horses were displayed in a Leavenworth store window. General Sheridan had ridden this horse twenty miles to the front and rallied his army at the battle of Winchester in October, 1864. Upon viewing the display of photographs, Mr. Henry reminisced: "Those are the pictures of Black Bill, the Winchester charger. They were taken over thirty years ago, and I remember it just as though it were only yesterday. One morning, in the spring of 1869, a four-mule ambulance came down from Fort Leavenworth to take me up. The driver said, 'General Sheridan wants a picture taken of his Winchester charger.' The horse, a large black one with three white feet, was brought out and placed close to the window of General Sheridan's library. I took two

pictures, one in which the charger was saddled and bridled, the other with only a bridle on. He was a powerful horse but did not seem to be fast. Nothing was known about the horse's breeding, nor did he have the appearance of a blooded animal. . . . General Sheridan was very proud of his charger and took as much care of him as I would of a diamond. There was an old groom that did nothing else but look after the horse. Although General Sheridan had been stationed at the fort for a year or two, I had never met him. The morning I went out to take the pictures, I supposed he was one of the officers in uniform. While taking the pictures I noticed a little Irishman moving around actively bossing things and telling where to place the horse . . . having his own way around the premises. I supposed he was a little Irish stable boss and paid scarcely any attention to him.

"We did not take pictures with dry plates in those times, and the pictures had to be developed immediately. I was in sort of a dark room preparing to develop when I noticed the Irishman standing just inside the door. Now you know there's a great danger that the least bit of light will spoil a picture, so I stopped and asked the man what he was doing there. He replied, 'It's my horse. Why shouldn't I see you make the pictures?' Well sir, I was surprised and said, 'Is this General Sheridan? I beg your pardon, General, I didn't know you.' He laughed and remained with me.

"While he closely watched the development of the pictures, we became good friends. I observed him closely after learning who he was. The Winchester charger died soon after General Sheridan left the fort, and later the general told me, 'These are the only pictures ever taken of him.'"

Harrison Putney (1864-1950)

Harrison Putney was only seven years old in October, 1871, when the great Chicago fire, the most destructive fire in American history, destroyed his father's wholesale furniture business, warehouse and all. David H. Putney's close friends persuaded him to move his family to Leavenworth, Kansas. Fred Harvey, who later started the restaurant chain of Harvey House, had recently built a new home in Leavenworth; and E. E. Henry, whom Putney had known in England, had long since established his photographic studio there. With good friends to encourage them the Putney family moved to Leavenworth.

Harry Putney's father bought three small houses in Leavenworth—one to live in and two to rent—but he never recovered from his great financial loss. David Putney died in about 1875, when Harrison was about ten years old.

E. E. Henry's wife had died in Oshawa, Canada, and after many years he married Mrs. Putney and raised the Putney children. Harrison Putney helped his stepfather in his studio, where he learned to shoot and retouch pictures. He became an excellent photographer, especially skilled at etching and eggshell retouching on glass negatives. He could remove an old-fashioned hat on a lady's portrait and replace it with a modern hairdo.

Harrison Putney was like his stepfather in that he had a pleasant disposition, a keen sense of humor, and a deep interest in photography. When Henry retired, Harrison Putney took over the Leavenworth studio until 1924, when he sold the Putney studio to Mary E. Everhard. Opening a small gift shop near his old photographic studio, Putney would often look in on Everhard to see how she was getting along.

Mary Everhard mentioned to Putney one afternoon, "I have just had a call to come and make pictures of a corpse, so I called my photographic competitor Mr. Stevenson, who was tickled to pieces."

Putney said, "Mary, you ought to do it. You only have to take one shot. They don't usually move."

Richard Stevenson (1824-1891)

Horace Stevenson (1867-1951)

At five o'clock August 18, 1940, Horace Stevenson locked his shop door for the final time. He was leaving for Los Angeles, California, and a well-earned retirement. Horace's father, pioneer photographer Richard Stevenson, had opened the business in 1858; today the oldest continuing photographic studio in Leavenworth was closed. No more tickling children's chins with that feathered wand; no more flicking India ink from a tooth brush onto a negative so that the printed picture would give the illusion of snow; no more painting with light the potbellied stoves of Leavenworth's Great Western Manufacturing Company.

Carrying his cameras and studio trappings, Richard Stevenson had come to Leavenworth, Kansas, on a steamboat in 1858. In those border war days Leavenworth wasn't a healthy place to be. The Planters Hotel, where Stevenson stayed, prevented slavery question fights by having two types of bartenders to cater to contentious guests from either side of the Mason-Dixon Line. When shooting began, offenders were hustled down the stone steps at the south entrance.

Undaunted, Richard Stevenson set up his photographic studio in four-year-old Leavenworth, on Fifth Street between Shawnee and Delaware. In 1884 his son Horace, at the age of seventeen, began helping his father in the studio. Horace learned his trade and, like his father, made excellent pictures. When his father died, in 1891, he continued as proprietor of the Stevenson Studio. Long before Horace Stevenson closed his studio, he arranged to place the Stevenson Studio negatives in the able hands of Mary Everhard, who continued to make prints available to the many Leavenworth customers served by the Stevensons.

Before leaving for his retirement in Los Angeles, Horace Stevenson remarked: "I'd rather live in Leavenworth than any place in the world, but I guess that much-advertised California climate will be good for me."

Mary E. Everhard (1887-1971)

she worked for the Cornish & Baker Studios of Kansas City, Missouri. Scanning the newspapers one morning in 1924, Mary found an advertisement: "For Sale—Putney Studio, Leavenworth, Kansas."

Purchasing her own studio was quite a task for Mary Everhard, but she managed and opened her studio that same year. With the Putney Studio and Everhard's own collection of excellent photographs came the collection of Henry Putney's glass negatives and later the combined negatives of pioneer photographers Richard and Horace Stevenson. Everhard researched, filed, cataloged, and preserved more than 40,000 negatives, 18 tons of glass.

In the 47 years she cared for this historic collection Everhard survived two locations and two tornadoes. Urged to have the negatives taken to the river Miss Everhard indignantly refused. She knew how important the negatives were, and she saved them for posterity.

Joseph E. Smith (1858-1922)

Joseph E. Smith had many businesses besides his photography. His office records were clear and complete. From diaries and letters Joseph Smith tells his story:

"I landed in Chicago, looking for a job. By chance I met up with a man who was looking for help in his photography business. I associated myself with him, and Chicago became my home base for the next two years [1880-1881].

"In the winter of 1882, I came to Socorro, New Mexico, with my friend Jim Leighton. It was sure frontier country in those days, but the life was fascinating, exciting, and wild with experiences, so I stayed.

"For several years I rode the

After attending a very select young ladies' finishing school in Philadelphia, Iowa-born Mary Everhard went on a Yankton College tour of Europe. Upon her return Everhard chose to live in New York City while she furthered her education in the field of photography. Courses and lectures from the top photographers of her day, Stieglitz and White, filled her time until she was able to land a job with a photographic studio in New York, which was famous for its portraits of children.

Miss Everhard gained a great deal of experience in taking pictures and retouching. In the 1920s range as a cowboy, and in those golden times, life was full of danger and hairbreadth experiences.

"My next venture was in the mines. Hard-rock mining at Kelly, New Mexico, a booming little mining camp near Magdalena, New Mexico. . . . It was only a stop-gap, so as soon as finances permitted, I sent east for a complete photography outfit—tent, drops, camera, and accessories. Setting myself up in the business as a sideline with the mine work. . . . I later quit the mines and came to Socorro, where I bought out the photography business of Edward Bass, about 1884. I made many side trips to the mining camps and cattle ranges to make pictures."

The summer of 1896 marked the end of Joseph Smith's picture-taking business. Through all his trials he managed to take incredible pictures of life in Socorro, New Mexico, and the surrounding areas. In the mines, above the mines, the cattle business, the sheep business, Indians, Mexicans, Chinese, railroad construction, the leisure life in Socorro, the occupations of all sorts, Mr. Smith provided us with a unique treasure of visual history in the southwestern United States.

Silas P. Melander (1853–c. 1915)

In the early history of Chicago photographers, the name most famous is Alexander Hessler. It was little wonder that Silas Melander was proud all his life that at the age of thirteen he had learned his trade from the great Alexander Hessler himself.

Born in Jonköping, Sweden, in 1853, Silas Melander moved with his family to Chicago in 1854. The Melander family were among the earliest Swedish immigrants to settle in Illinois. In 1866, after he had obtained some elementary schooling, Melander became Hessler's photographer's assistant. A few years later he established his first gallery, at 131 Lake Street, where he remained until the Chicago fire of 1871. At the time of the fire he saved not only his own possessions but many of Hessler's as well.

Mr. Melander's studio catered to Chicago society, and he had an extensive file of stereo negatives from which his customers made cards for a mail-order business. Expeditions to photograph for a new series of stereo cards took Mr. Melander and his brother Louis Melander all over the world.

In 1879 Mr. Melander built the photographic studio at 208 Ohio Street, known as "Chicago's Finest," and he remained there until he retired.

Seneca Ray Stoddard (1844-1917)

Three of the greatest nineteenth-century photographers were born within a hundred miles of one another in upstate New York: Mathew B. Brady (c. 1823-1896) near Lake George in Warren County; William H. Jackson (1843-1942) in Peru, Clinton County; and Seneca Ray Stoddard (1844-1917) in Wilton, Saratoga County.

Brady and his staff of talented photographers gained their fame by taking more than 3,500 superb Civil War battle pictures and camp scenes. Jackson's fame was soundly based on his memorable photographs and paintings of the West.

Stoddard was unquestionably the most versatile of the group. Along with his success as an editor and magazine publisher he was also a talented artist with ink, oils, and watercolors. He was also an inventor, a sensitive poet, a witty writer, and one of the most widely traveled men of his time. His eloquent lectures, illustrated by his unique and carefully tinted stereopticon slides, provided many entertaining evenings for Adirondacks vacationers.

Though the Adirondacks were Stoddard's favorite photographing area, he traveled extensively in the West and the Southwest, in Alaska, Canada, and Cuba, and through most of Europe and North Africa.

On the night of July 17, 1892, Stoddard, accompanied by R. B. Burchard of New York, left Glens Falls by train for Montreal, the starting point for their long-planned trip to Alaska. Both looked forward to an interesting trip, a journey that would provide the photographer with the necessary material for another lecture program. Late the next afternoon, they boarded a Canadian Pacific train for the six-day trip to Tacoma, Washington. Their first attempt at taking pictures was at Regina, where Indian teepees dotted the plains. The Indians gathered around the station, the men in their gaudy blankets and feathers and the women loaded with beadwork and articles for sale.

When Stoddard revealed his camera, the Indians regarded it with superstitious awe. Singling out one group of three braves, Stoddard tried to get them to stay together long enough to snap the shutter, but they scattered like rabbits. The women hastily covered their faces with blankets and pulled their children under with them.

Later at Calgary, Canada, they were able to visit a Sarcee reservation ten miles to the south. Members of this tribe made violent objections to having their pictures taken, so Stoddard had either to bribe them or trip the shutter stealthily. Most of the Indians succumbed to the offer of money for posing. The scale ranged from fifty cents for the common brave up to five dollars, the princely sum extorted by the surly chief Bullhead.

The WEST

an american experience

During the course of his journey the photographer made about a thousand exposures. His greatest disappointment came when he discovered—too late to be able to do anything about it—that his "elephant" camera was a total failure. The huge piece of equipment, reputed to be the largest camera in the world at that time, had been built under his supervision especially for Alaska's scenery and was designed to take a negative measuring 20 by 49 inches. Fortunately, the mechanical defects were corrected later on, so the innovation was not a complete fiasco.

When the mammoth camera failed him, Stoddard relied on the two smaller cameras he had packed for the trip. The results of the Alaskan journey were shown at the Glens Falls Lyceum to a crowded house. The executive committee of the Lyceum later sponsored a lecture series by Seneca Ray Stoddard, a versatile camera artist.

1 Jumping-off Place

A jumping-off place presumes a past and a future. One can only jump off from somewhere to somewhere. Thus the jumping-off place is necessarily a fusion of the past and the future. It represents a hope and a promise and a panorama of the breadth of human passion and human need.

In the jumping-off place we see all of the vast horizon of human aspiration. Here are the hopeful, the defeated, the young, the burdened, the honored, the despised. Some have come secure in the knowledge that they will make their futures, and there are those who are unaware of what awaits them or of what it will take to survive. We see in this founding river city everything that beckoned them to an unknown future. These are the people who came to the prairie—amazed, bewildered, delighted, and intimidated by it. They came by river—the ancient method for forming cities—and they came by the new railroads, filling the city with every type of wandering human being: bearded frontiersmen, portly merchants, confidence men, riverboat captains, Indians in from the western plains, soldiers newly arriving and newly departing. Here were the sounds and shrieks of riverboats and the whistles of trains, the grinding of boxcar wheels, the bellowing of animals, the shrill cries of children at play.

Leavenworth, Kansas, demonstrated the noisy panoply of a forming city, and it was this beehive of frontier activity that held the attention of our Leavenworth photographer E. E. Henry. Almost entirely this was not a visual world, as ours is today; few had the ability to record the world they lived in. This, indeed, was the special province of the artist, the lithographer, and the wood engraver. They filled the world with their own romantic bias, attractive and dubious.

Look at the ornate, graceful detailing of the heavy railway car from which a woman with her fur muff and her carefully coiled umbrella is descending. Notice the stencils that decorate the wooden cars and the grime that coexists with this attempt to bring beauty and delicacy into a harsh world. Dressed in her best, presenting all her finery, hoping that her arrival in this new land—she is not altogether sure of her reception or the character of this land at which she has arrived—may meet the expectations that buoyed her in the long journey from the East.

Delaware Street, Leavenworth, 1867, appears to spring from the Missouri River waterfront.

Opposite: Commission houses line up along Levee Street, Leavenworth's first street of commerce, in 1862. Photographer, E. E. Henry.

Through the photography of E. E. Henry we see this jumping-off place, toehold of an unknown continent. It was a city of curious contrast, boasting fashionable city streets with decorated buildings of two and three stories, housing every type of commercial enterprise, ending abruptly at the river bank or the endless prairie. There is a bizarre quality about a city that seems to end nowhere and for no reason. And yet Leavenworth is the typical jumping-off place.

The newly completed Stillings pontoon bridge, opened in 1882, was the scene of much excitement for the people of Leavenworth, particularly the local children. *Photographer, E. E. Henry.*

Photographer Harry Putney's dog playing in the Missouri River at Leavenworth in 1882. Putney stopped the action with an early Eastman Kodak box camera.

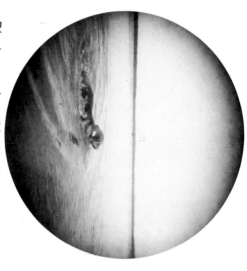

Many images in these photographs merit our special attention. Examine carefully the eternal spring delight of young children playing on the levee, on the banks of the Missouri River. Such a picture in life may have sparked the fertile imagination of Samuel Langhorne Clemens to produce the American classic *Tom Sawyer.* Here is the innocence of rural youth responding to an ever-changing activity that marked the entrance from this river city to the widening West.

The greatness of photography is that it allows for the widest participation and perception of each viewer. Pictures ask many questions—in this case, preeminently, "Which of these Tom Sawyers is *the* Tom Sawyer?" Is it the youngster with his checked shirt leaning on the rail? The delicate one with the tight pants and the straw hat, like the hat that Tom sailed into the air on at least one occasion? The little boy without shoes who is hoping that no one will notice that he is walking barefooted on the splintered planks? The older boy looking at the camera? Which of them brings to this view of the Missouri River the excitement, the anticipation, the unsullied boyhood innocence and joy that Mark Twain wrote of in the odyssey of Tom Sawyer? Hannibal, Missouri, is not far from the actual scene of this Leavenworth photograph. Some documents are so timeless that they perpetuate a time, a place, and a feeling, transcending the normal function of a photograph, which is merely to record and document. In this riverbank scene we have all the warmth and richness, the vitality, the shimmering exuberance of life in the 1860s in the Missouri River town of Leavenworth.

Particularly worthy of close examination is the Leavenworth Railroad Station of the newly arrived Kansas Pacific Railway (following page). Here can be seen an extraordinary jumble—of merchandise in bags and in barrels, still jammed into overloaded flat cars, waiting

to be off-loaded into delivery wagons. It suggests men unable to de-
cide which to unload first, of all the materials needed to outfit and
provide housing for the many who flocked to this prairie city or who
planned to leave, forging ever westward. For the city was not only a
terminus; it was also a gateway. All of the confusion, all of the inde-
scribable bustle of activity that supported, and was, this coming and
going was evident in the interchange of people and goods between
the riverboats and the new railway.

Boxcars stenciled KPRW date this scene of Leavenworth's first railway depot as 1867. The station was located at Olive Street, and the viewer is facing north from the South Esplanade. Photographer, E. E. Henry.

Above: In the midst of the back-breaking work of settlement, there was still time for leisure. These bachelors are in their hotel room at the Planters Hotel, Leavenworth, 1869. The Planters was known as the best hotel north of St. Louis. *Photographer, E. E. Henry.*

Upper right: In the space of just one year, 1869, 175 steamboats landed at Leavenworth, Kansas. The St. Louis and Omaha packet Silver Bow was one of them. If you look closely between the smokestacks, you can see the cannon used to ward off river pirates or announce an arrival. *Photographer, E. E. Henry.*

One cannot comprehend the revealed impatience that lies behind the faces of the men sitting in the room of the Planters Hotel without understanding the nature of the opening West. Reading Leavenworth's papers and journals or looking blankly into the camera, they wait for the arrival or the departure of wagon trains, railway trains, steamboats—events to mark an end to their stay in this terminus, this brawling, growing gateway to a new and sprawling country. And for some it was all too much. In the men's faces one can find some idea of the consequences of beginning to build a new life, of unexpected waits, of curious boredom: men fell victim of disorientation, anxiety, and isolation. Among them, of course, came the men of God. Certain that God had no color, Mr. Moses Dixon appears certain also of his work, his devotion, his reward, his kinship with his God—but uncertain of his relationship with his fellow men.

The Kansas Pacific Railroad pulling out of Leavenworth's depot, 1869.
Photographer, E. E. Henry.

After the Civil War many black people moved north to Kansas. Pictured is the Reverend Moses Dixon, Leavenworth, 1878. Photographer, E. E. Henry.

Mr. Gird, a pioneer of Leavenworth. Photographer, E. E. Henry.

Leavenworth had many fine hotels. The National Hotel, photographed in 1884 by E. E. Henry, had not only a dining room but a Turkish bath.

14

Judge Robert Crozier and his family pose for a portrait in front of their Leavenworth home in 1869.

Mr. L. Moore and his wife moved to Kansas as part of the "Exoduster" movement from the South. This family portrait was taken in Leavenworth, 1892. Photographer, Harry Putney.

This unknown Leavenworth lawyer, probably a politician as well, had his picture taken for use on an 1874 campaign poster. *Photographer, Richard Stevenson.*

More than most, this photography portrays indelibly a portion of the national heritage. It is hard not to be impressed with the ease with which newly arriving visitors built their own world, establishing themselves, almost recklessly, wherever they found themselves. In this photograph is the shaded solemnity of a law office—the commercial necessity—with all the trappings of business that go with a law office in any of the ancient buildings on Boyleston Street in Boston, Massachusetts. Except that it isn't Boston. It is Leavenworth, Kansas, in 1860.

Land deeds, title tracing, legal services of all kinds could be handled at the law office of Endres and Atwood. Photographer, Horace Stevenson.

There is something immensely appealing about the joyful innocence of workers who take pleasure in posing in the costumes, and with the tools, of their trade. Theirs is an affirmation and a celebration of work, not to mention a kind of wonder at their own courage; armed only with a determination to build and subdue the land, they are blithely taking on an implacable wilderness. It is a recognition of the fact that, for them, their future and the future of the territories to which they plan to go are dependent upon their labor—not as hired laborers but as free workers ready to wrestle with nature and fashion from it the world of their dreams and their aspirations.

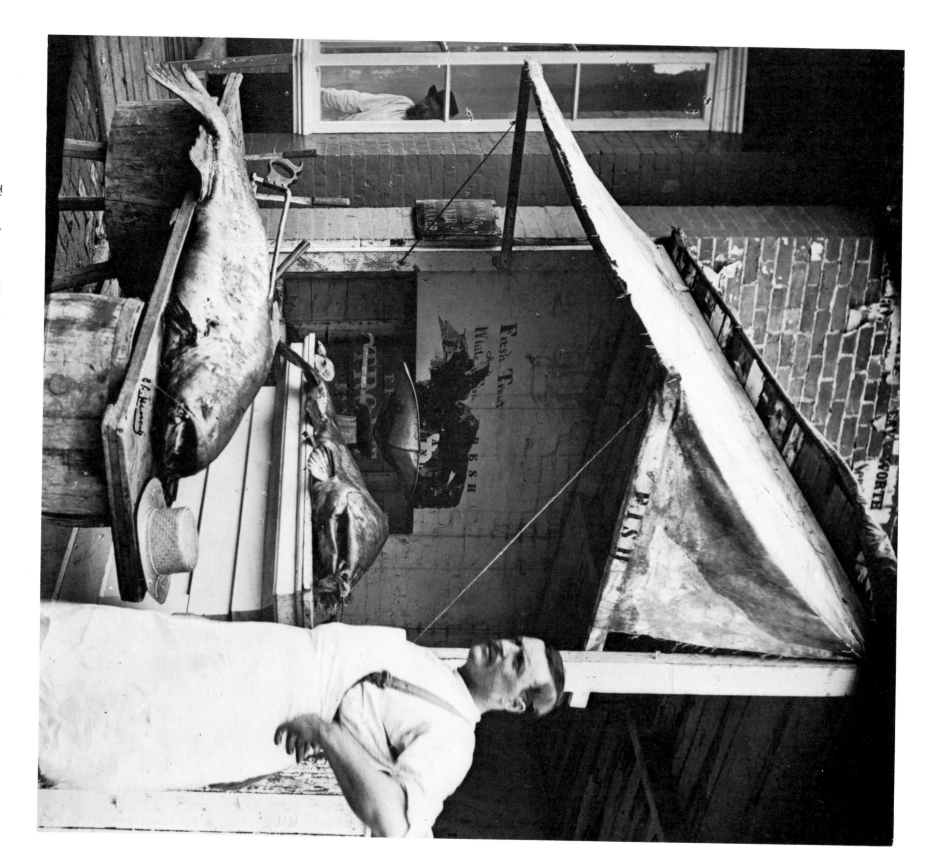

Above: Linemen for the Insley Telegraph Company, 1882. The first telephone system was set up in Leavenworth in 1879.

Opposite: A channel catfish caught in the Missouri River near Leavenworth in 1869 was brought to Ed Dustin to be sold. The Dustin Brothers Fish Market was located at 422 Shawnee Street. Photographer, E. E. Henry.

Painter Mr. D. L. Ryan, 1890.
Photographer, Horace Stevenson.

Journalist Mr. James, 1892.
Photographer, Horace Stevenson.

Richard McCormack, bricklayer, 1892. Photographer, Horace Stevenson.

Carpenters, 1885. Photographer, Harry Putney.

Mr. Clark, paperhanger, 1885.
Photographer, Harry Putney.

Miss Weaver and nurses, 1888.
Photographer, Horace Stevenson.

Mr. Bert Nelves and company, coal miners, 1884. Photographer, E. E. Henry.

There was work to do in Leavenworth, and these are some of the men and women who got it done. Photographer Horace Stevenson used a triple exposure in some of the photographs to take three different pictures of the same person on one negative.

Postman, 1887.
Photographer, Horace Stevenson.

Circus performers came from all over the world to purchase equipment from the C. W. Parker Company, Leavenworth. The Great Layton tries out his new slack wire, 1885. Photographer, Harry Putney.

Mr. H. Lissik whirls a baton for the benefit of Harry Putney's camera (1886).

24

Publicity shot of the Lissiks. The act started when Mrs. Lissik ran a sword through a large wooden clock. The clock's sides fell away to reveal the flag and a bird cage, which Mr. Lissik balanced on his mandolin. Photographer, Harry Putney.

Pat Doyle, circus entertainer, dressed as a harlequin.

Not all aspects of life were wholly frightening—to speak of streetcars now is to speak of nostalgia. No one can forget the thrill and delicious terror of that first ride on a streetcar—rumbling its way down the street, shaking, moving, making strange noises, imparting strange sensations and the sense of power that comes from being carried relentlessly forward—and so it is easy to understand the determination of every one of these children to cling, regardless of any danger, to this favorite vehicle of the time. Locomotion was the magic that suffused the otherwise commonplace life of small towns a hundred years ago with excitement.

Leavenworth's first electric rail streetcar, 1902, featured open cars for summer and closed cars for winter. The streetcar operated between the Wadsworth Soldiers' Home in Fort Leavenworth and Leavenworth City. Photographer, Horace Stevenson.

Delaware Street, Leavenworth, Kansas, in the 1860s is a study in contrasts. Conceive of a main street that is dust in the summertime and mud in the wintertime. Think of a street that sees only horses, wagons, and oxen. Think of a street where the sidewalks are wooden plank laid upon the dirt. Think of a street where wooden buildings of ancient vintage sit side by side with brick buildings bedecked with the most modern in pressed-iron decoration. That was Delaware Street, a mélange of businessmen—and others—who lined the streets, determined to make their fortune from those who passed through or settled in the town. Two gentlemen, a Mr. Crew and a Mr. Morgan, sell books. A Miss Wilson is a dressmaker. If you needed a carriage, Mr. S. L. North would rent you one. And if on your return you were dusty, you simply

could go next door and have a bath (Baeder). Mr. Rothschild, next door, would sell you hats, caps, and furs. And just next door to Mr. Rothschild's there is a cigar and tobacco store—should you think a cigar refreshing toward the end of the day. If it is necessary to have an indelible printed record of your journey here to Leavenworth, Mr. S. Dodsworth, a printer and binder, can whip up any notice. Across the street, Mr. Scott and Mr. Woodruff sell fruits. A Singer sewing machine can be bought, and a Mr. Flesher sells the dry goods you as a frontier homemaker need to make your clothes. You can buy furniture, mattresses, pianos. There is even a dentist for those with ailing teeth—a man whose skills are much called into use, quite probably, because of the presence of the Western Candy Factory.

The preceding page shows an extremely rare wide view of Delaware Street, 1869, taken on two separate negatives. The areas within the crop marks on the contact print on the opposite page were enlarged with extremely sharp lenses to magnify a small section of the street (shown above) and focus on the door of C. Clark's china, glass, and cutlery shop (opposite page). Photographer, E. E. Henry.

Clark's china shop was very popular with the ladies of Leavenworth. He brought refinement and gentility to the town with his fancy imported wares. *Photographer, E. E. Henry.*

The activity of Delaware Street is poignantly revealed in these vivid 1869 closeups. Douglas Phillips, grandfather to the author, worked as a bookkeeper at the Stutsman and Keene Merchant Tailors, 110 Delaware Street (see detail, opposite page). *Photographer, E. E. Henry.*

Above: Staff members of the Commercial Printing Office, 23 Delaware Street, strike up their pose for photographer E. E. Henry in 1867.

Opposite top: Newspapers were vital to the economy of the small plains towns of the West. Advertisements for land and business opportunities filled the pages of the lively evening newspaper, the Bulletin. Photographer, E. E. Henry.

Opposite bottom: Fast deliveries were needed for the many commission houses in Leavenworth, 1869. The expressman is waiting in front of Samuel Dodsworth Stationers, which operates today in Kansas City, Missouri. Photographer, E. E. Henry.

Attendants guard the underground arsenal at Fort Leavenworth, Kansas, 1869. Photographer, E. E. Henry.

34

If nothing else in America, especially in the West, people *moved*, and as we can see, they were, from earliest ages, caught up in that particular American social necessity: mobility. Leavenworth, Kansas, was not only a commercial and cultural center for the embryonic West; it was also a reminder that this frontier was one not to be subdued only by hoes, rakes, sweat, and determination. There were people we called "enemies" to be considered: the prior inhabitants. Others had lived around Leavenworth, and throughout the nation, long before the white man came. Men had decided that they could not live in common: soldiers, an army, were never far from the frontiersmen. This frontier *was* going to be subdued—militarily when necessary. Leavenworth was the forming area for a massive army and all of its accouterments—the center of a military world so desperately needed by the new settlers. In Leavenworth could be found the military prisons, the barracks, the soldiers—a massive collection of all of the materiel necessary to guarantee that the land's subjugation by the settlers would be carried on in relative peace in the face of the determination of its original settlers to drive them out.

Left, this page: Private J. W. Gardner of the Ninth Cavalry, Fort Leavenworth. Frederick Remington painted this famous cavalry in an 1880 battle charge on the western plains. Photographer, E. E. Henry.

Opposite page: Spanish-American War trooper Hagedorn draws a bead on photographer Harry Putney, 1903. Regardless of the angle from which the photograph is viewed, Hagedorn always aims at the viewer. Photographer, Harry Putney.

One of the many cavalry units that paraded on the grounds of Fort Leavenworth during the period just after the Spanish-American War, c. 1900. Photographer, E. E. Henry.

Above: Tracks along the Missouri River bluffs just outside of Leavenworth, 1869. This stretch of track is a fine example of the rough-hewn ties cut from the roadside forests by early railroad workers. Photographer, E. E. Henry.

Opposite: Steamboat Luella pulling away from Leavenworth. The Luella was bound for Weston, Missouri, one of the many small towns dotting the eastern bank of the Missouri River.

There was a grandeur, too, about the Missouri River steamer. The sight of its black clouds was the sure reminder of the existence of another world, outside the West, miles down river. At night its fierce fires were the same assurance that Leavenworth was not alone, that the larger world would come to visit. And come the world did—with people, with supplies, with the flavor and excitement of those who

manned the vessels, with all of the pleasures of places known but never visited. The steamer was an invitation to the world; it was a ticket to the world. Indeed the steamer, before the railroad, was the chief link in the forging of the chain of national unity. The steamers tied all the scattered communities together, regionally and even nationally, developing an awareness of a large conglomeration-of cities, of people, and of people linked together.

It is almost impossible to visualize the curious combination of the new, the advanced, the old, and the primitive that characterized the border town in transition at a time of crisis in the founding nation. Would you expect to find a Shawnee Street in border Kansas? You could, and would. Shawnee Street was like all other streets in Leavenworth—wood plank sidewalks, mud, great width (to accommodate the procession of ox trains and wagon trains that made their way in and out). In Leavenworth, too, there was even a typical Western

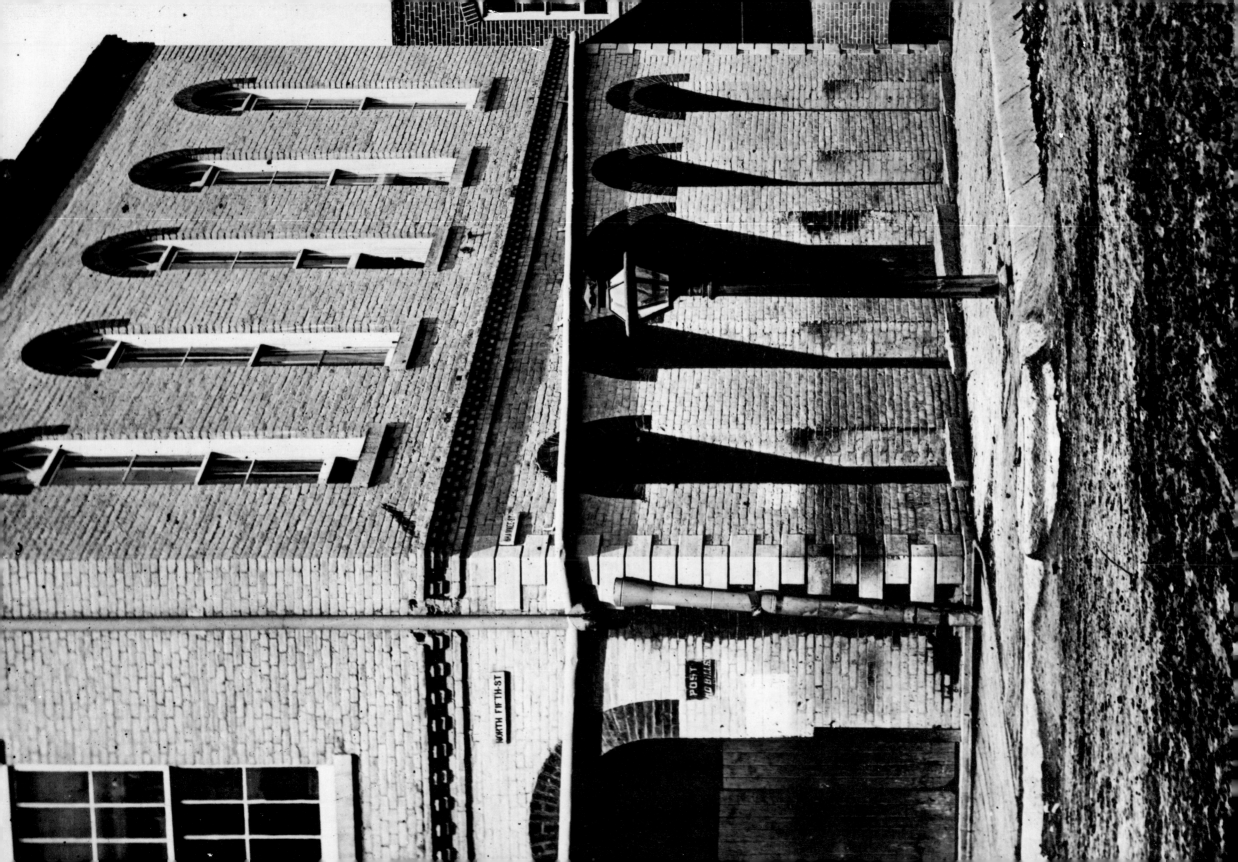

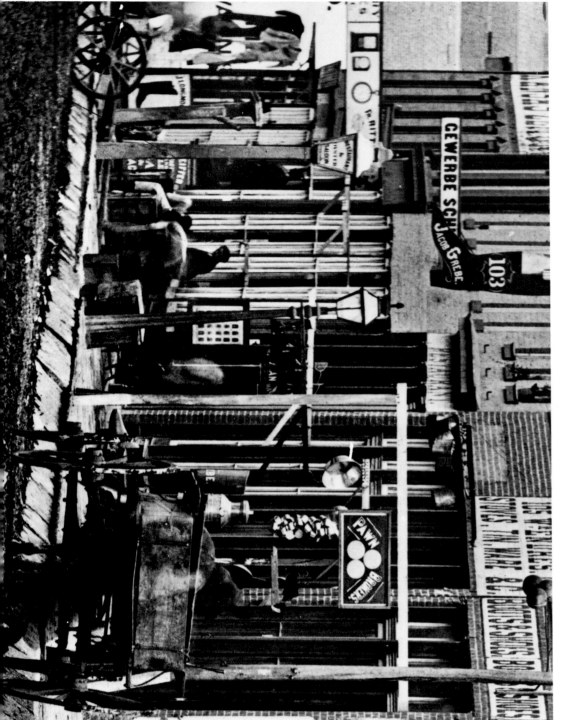

Foldout inside: PANORAMA, SHAWNEE STREET,
LEAVENWORTH, KANSAS

saloon, the immortal Star of the West of Leavenworth, Kansas, one to rival the Long Branch Saloon of Dodge City. Stereotypical, one says. But above the saloon lies the office of the Kansas Free Press, and next to it was the Probate Court; not far away, Leavenworth, like every other city in the growing West determined to establish its sophistication, supported its Delmonico Restaurant. Aware of the reputation and excitement of New York, Kansas more than asserted its willingness to emulate such a capital on the sprawling border frontier that marked Missouri Territory in the 1860s.

Especially sharp, handcrafted lenses used by Leavenworth photographer E. E. Henry enabled us to enlarge minute details from various portions of the magnificent panorama of Shawnee Street, shot in 1869. The small pictures below are the exact size of Mr. Henry's original negatives. White crop marks on the contact prints indicate the image areas from which the enlargements were made.

Fourth and Delaware Streets was the site of the First National Bank of Leavenworth, still in business today. A fragment of the sign advertising E. E. Henry's studio is visible.

To appreciate Leavenworth, Kansas, one must know that it was the beginning of "out there," as the popular phrase went. "Out there" was no particular place. "Out there" meant *everywhere*—everywhere where the many Wests lay fallow in innocence, to be discovered by the wandering settler.

It was possible to find whatever one aspired to in this immense West. There was the West of Montana, of Arizona, of New Mexico, of Colorado, of Iowa, of Idaho. There was the agricultural West; there was the ranching West. There was the West for miners; there was the West waiting to be logged. There was the West where winds blew strong, and there was the West of gentle blue skies. There was the West cut through by massive rivers on whose banks cities could be built. There were the plains where locomotives would be able to thunder unchecked for miles. All of these Wests, and others besides, awaited the settlers who used Leavenworth and the other jumping-off places as their terminus and point of departure. Each in his turn arrived and settled or went on or both, in response to some inner compulsion to grab a share of the American dream, to claim the promise of joy and the reward he felt was his by birth. For most, some part of the dream was won temporarily, not forever, but no one believed that luck could not change. There was always another Leavenworth, another river, another mine, to try. Thus what we see in these photographs—the faces, the lives, the clothes, the manner of living that marked these settlers, a record of life that exists unvarnished, unblemished—is a mixture of life and concern, optimism and fear, determination and defeat. It is all the characteristics of humanity almost naively flaunted—not self-protectively covered by a veneer of indifference or sophistication—by an uncompromising people, and captured by the curious but sympathetic eye that is the hallmark of the itinerant photographer in the American West in the nineteenth century.

2 Where clean Winds Blew

Of all the contrivances man has developed in his age-long struggle to subdue nature, the windmill that is so much a part of Europe and that served so magnificently for centuries was seldom at first a feature of the American landscape. It was only late in the nineteenth century that an American version was developed to assist man in his search for water—and typically it appeared on the great wind-swept ranches of the West. Yet there were untypical, "European" mills, too, such as this one (opposite page) near Lawrence, Kansas. Untypical in construction and style, working its way with the free power of the wind for centuries, it stands in noble disrepair, a curious monument to the melting pot that brought the skills and the techniques that enabled settling Americans to subdue the plains and build the West.

Such windmills were aberrations; they were inefficient, did not do their share of work, were not value for money. Instead, the "clean" American windmill asserted itself, reflecting an American inventiveness that copied the newness of the West. Another example was the railroad, which, wherever it made its way, marked a major turning point in the story of the settlement of the West. Before the railroad were years of the enforced isolation, the bitter loneliness, the unrelieved tedium, the terror and hopelessness of living separated from unknown neighbors by miles of flat prairie. Life seldom provided the contact and the comfort, the excitement and the stimulation that mankind needs to grow. After the railroad came, the loneliness was broken forever by the thin, seemingly endless ribbon of iron on which the early locomotives of the nineteenth century made their smoking, shrieking way across the plains. To document this change is to document a major moment in the life of the people who discovered how they could stretch a hand across their country and find it joined at either end by willing Americans interested in their future, interested in their fate.

We in America today live with a kind of sophisticated loneliness that we call alienation. It is real and it is grievous. But it prevents us, perhaps, from understanding the poignant kind of physical loneliness that comes from living in a territory where few others live, where moving from one location to another is a major event involving planning, expense, and risk beyond our ability to describe, let alone imagine.

The clean winds once propelled this wonderful old mill standing sentinel at Lawrence, Kansas, in 1890. Photographer unknown.

Steaming across the hot, barren prairie, the St. Paul-Minneapolis-Manitoba railway cuts through the seemingly endless Reo River Valley in 1886. Amateur photographer, Irwin Rew.

Watching the windmill turn and the water tank leak, the people wait for a far-off train at Dillon, Montana, 1885. Photo, Dillon Studio.

However, this photograph depicts a scene that typifies the loneliness of the universal peasant, the farmer—call him what you will—anywhere in the world. The huddled people protecting themselves from the biting cold of a Dillon, Montana, morning are almost shapeless. They seem not to be people, as though the land does not welcome them, as though their presence is a violation of the eternal relationship between the land and the sky. And this unwelcome, psychologically depressing barrier to settlement in the new land was the daily fare of those who were determined to subdue the West; if, in addition, they came from foreign lands and had also to transform themselves into Americans, the cost to them would be incalculable. Only a part of the hardship is captured by the camera, but even through this limited medium we are able to sense in this vivid image the immense isolation and estrangement from the rest of the world that was the lot of those who came to the experience we call the American West.

Of course, not everywhere was the land as hard as at Dillon, Montana (though most places were). There were places in the West—not many to be sure—where the settlers arrived not as strangers, not as first settlers, not alone, places where they were welcomed as neighbors, new settlers, friends. Such places linger long in the memories of those who settled there. While the people spoke a different language, were a different color, built different kinds of homes, ate different kinds of foods, and had different responses to similar experiences, they were people who, in their warmth and in their grace, provided the settlers with all they needed to know to live in these strange lands. These were people who taught the visitors how to live in the deserts, who provided them with the skills they needed to live in the cold, who showed them the fruits and vegetables they could and could not eat and taught them to prepare meat in ways that enabled the settlers to flourish. These were the other Americans whose future we have not yet linked with our own as one common people in one common land.

It has become almost a cliché to call Santa Fe, New Mexico, the jewel of the Southwest; but, as is usually the case, a saying becomes a cliché because it is true. Here we see Santa Fe when it was not so much of a "jewel," in our terms, in its infancy—in size if not in age. The towering Cathedral can be seen looming over the horizon when it was the highest structure in this city of Mexicans, ancient in its tradition and culture, wise in its humanity, ever ready to welcome any stranger, any visitor—the founding source and the beginning of the richness of the whole Southwest of the United States.

Elfego Baca, the famous sheriff of Socorro, New Mexico, must have walked past this Socorro livery stable (1886) as a young man.

Opposite: The shade and the cool adobe shelter protected the settlers from the scorching New Mexico sun. Only the puppy doesn't seem to mind the Santa Fe heat. Photographer unknown.

New Mexico was the ranching West. But cattle, a synonym for gold, require only the support of little towns. Socorro, New Mexico, was one such town. An ancient town, home of the Hopi, the Apache, the Comanche, Socorro was on the route of the Spanish explorers and the last important stop before the Jornada del Muerto—the "journey of death"—a trail dreaded in the olden days because of the long, almost endless, waterless trek from El Paso over the southwestern desert.

One of many ox teams that trampled the Socorro streets, 1888. Three wagons filled to the brim with goods needed this team of twelve dependable oxen. Photographer, Joseph E. Smith.

Socorro was one of the little towns where settlers built a courthouse and business enterprises. Wood, brick, and adobe buildings stood side by side. The raising and selling of hay was a major concern. A livery stable was as commonplace as a drugstore is today. Even horses and burros could not transport the quantity of goods necessary to sustain life and commerce, and oxen, the ancient beasts of burden, were brought successfully into play and became as much a part of the scene in the streets of Socorro as the blistering sun.

Sheep on a ranch near Socorro provided the warm clothing and blankets needed for the cold winter months. Photographer, Joseph E. Smith.

The Santa Fe Railroad tracks met the "Trail's End Pens" at Magdalena, New Mexico, 1887. Cattlemen from the southwest corner of New Mexico and as far as Arizona regarded the pens as the eye of the needle for their immense five- to ten-mile-wide stock drives. Photographer, Joseph E. Smith.

As its name implies, Socorro offered succor to a weary mankind, an oasis in a blinding and arid desert. Here the men and women who came from the East, together with their Mexican neighbors, developed sheep rearing to a highly successful degree and built corrals out of lumber brought from the mountains for the "trails' end pens," such as those at Magdalena, New Mexico, for the cattle that were to be shipped to the eastern markets, representative samples of the staple for which the United States became famous throughout the world—an endless supply of the very best meat obtainable. The display of meat for sale in a Socorro market was almost beyond belief.

In 1886 Joseph E. Smith shot this wonderful interior of a Socorro, New Mexico, meat market with two dry-plate negatives. The individual prints were joined to make one wide view. Perhaps the butcher in this picture got his patriotic idea from the 1876 Centennial Exposition in Philadelphia, where meat displays featured American flags pinned on all kinds of meats.

Socorro, like all other towns where men must live and die, was not without its own successful efforts to sustain the richness of play, the release from tension, the avoidance of the difficulties and hardships of desert life. Real abandon can be seen in the photograph of people celebrating Halloween. The ambience of excitement that was typical of the ability of those who settled the West to work hard and to play hard can only be hinted at by the inventiveness of the costumes, the suggestion of the whirling couples, the heat, the noise of the music, and the vivid figures in the left foreground.

Photographer Joseph E. Smith caught the leisurely spirit of a costume party in the Garcia Opera House, Socorro, 1887. Magnesium powder exploded in Mr. Smith's flash powder gun, creating the light and acting as a fast shutter to stop the movement of the whirling figures.

The photograph of the destruction of the town of Park City, New Mexico (following page), recalls to mind that ancient evil with which all frontier settlements had to concern themselves, the devastating effects of fire in towns built of wood. In this photograph the residents of Park City, attempting to recover their few possessions that have escaped the ravages of fire, stand in the cold light of morning gazing with dismay upon the destruction of years of effort, facing the painful necessity of beginning again, of snatching back again from the desert a proven and sustaining way of life.

After saving as much of their property as possible, residents of Park City, New Mexico, settle down on a store countertop to wait out the smoldering fire, 1886.

Ranching, of course, was not the only pursuit. For western settlers, diversification was as necessary as breathing. The land would provide only what it could yield. It was known that the land was rich in minerals. Mining took every form, permanent and transient. The little tent of the sourdough prospector, determined to pursue his hunch, his luck, dotted the landscape almost as widely as did the pine trees in the foothills of the mountains he explored.

There were the larger towns set up to exploit the many lodes that were found to yield the desired riches, and the hopeful towns that offered classic expositions of the determination to believe in the one good break.

Any makeshift shack would do for the sourdough miners at Kelly, New Mexico, in the 1880s. Most Kelly miners spent their days in the hard-rock mines and their nights in the saloons. Photographer, Joseph E. Smith.

Construction in Magdalena, New Mexico, a mining town in the Magdalena Mountains near Socorro. The paint on half of the building on the right makes it appear half in shadow (1880). Photographer, Edward A. Bass.

Opposite top: The miners had a drink and cooled their heels outside Socorro's Walton Saloon (1887). Photographer, Joseph E. Smith.

Opposite bottom: Smith's remarkable perception as an early photo-journalist provoked him to catch a typical card game in the South-west, 1886.

Saloon in Kelly, New Mexico. Refreshment for men and horses. Photographer, Joseph E. Smith.

In Socorro, one can see the town merchants, the attorneys, the middle class, enjoying themselves in front of the social center, the town saloon. Forbidden to women, the saloons took every form, from luxurious wooden buildings with verandas and chairs to wretched wooden buildings hastily thrown up, hand-lettered signs and all, to provide—at expensive prices—the means to forget the drudgery and the bitterness of the never-ending search for gold. When gold was found there were those who were prepared to lose it in games of chance that were, more often than not, rigged. To find pictures of westerners gambling is to witness a phenomenon that was as commonplace then as walking and eating. The diversions were few; skill at cards and the possibility of changing one's luck at the toss of the dice were ever present.

Early Socorro, New Mexico, saloon, 1880s.

Finery on the frontier was neither necessary nor known, and yet there was dignity. The taking of a family photograph was an act of immense pride. It was a recording in time of all of the noble motivations that enabled people to endure the privations of hard living. It recorded the building of small adobe shacks, unwindowed, undoored in many cases; it showed the endless labor needed to provide the food required by man and beast. Men endured the blistering sun, the inability to provide education, the lack of churches, the lack of neighborly comfort—all of these hardships were the day-to-day lot, and

they were accepted cheerfully or otherwise—so long as, in most cases, there was a maintenance, in their own minds usually, of dignity based on the recognition of the forthrightness of their efforts. The taking of a photograph codified such feelings; this family expresses that magnificent moment for a visiting photographer in Socorro.

Well-tended horses, the best means of transportation in Socorro, are included in this 1888 family portrait. The ranchhouse was made of special adobe mud bricks. *Photographer, Joseph E. Smith.*

Such moments of dignity were repeated throughout the West. The configuration was always different, the impulse always the same. Here is a family of five: the man, about forty but bearded and aged beyond his years, standing in front of a wooden cabin, built painfully and with difficulty but still with the graceful touch of a birdcage at the door, providing the sound of life. Here are the sober, somewhat somber visages of people—living in isolation with a dream of a farm and a community that could support their aspirations for a life free from feudal tyranny in the new land, the new West.

Opposite: The refinements of a window curtain and lumber from a sawmill were just the beginning for this family, located near Denver. Photographer unknown.

Below: Wood was plentiful even for the shake roof of this family home just outside Denver, Colorado, in the 1880s. Photographer unknown.

It was a procession of predictable faces, not always different in their configuration. There were hundreds of bearded, sad-eyed men, women dressed in black, unable to place their hands in suitable positions, unskilled in the art of posing, families determined to record for a brief moment the difficulty, the hardship, the loneliness, and the glory of their lives: those who came to found a West that could survive and could grow.

Homemade bread, corn on the cob, and other good things to eat grace the table on the Parmenter ranch, near Denver, Colorado, 1889. Photographer unknown.

Happily, their success and joy also were captured, in the celebration of harvest, of good fortune, of bringing together families from the old country and the new, and such scenes as the years went by and the century drew to a close became more commonplace. More often, people celebrated the determination and the success of those who had come before them to guarantee that the foundations for this kind of life were built solidly and successfully.

There were no stores, no supermarkets in the American West. Few supplies were brought in to the the far reaches of the West. It was the land, the land itself, to which the people turned for everything required to sustain life. Those who could hunt, did; those who did not know how, learned. The gun became more a means of maintaining life than it was of taking it. In every western family there was the hunter, and he would embark on hunting trips. The capacity to provide was a human quality more desired than charm. In the summer, when the weather was good, the food of the summer was put away in jars to carry the family through bitter winters. The labor of canning and packing and putting away provisions for the difficult winter to come was a part of life, so ordinary a task that it was rarely recorded. During those winters the inability to sustain one's own products meant death—cold, isolated, bitter death.

Typical of the hunters of his time, this man seems to have bagged what he needed for his supper table. *Photographer, Silas Melander.*

Deer abounded, but they were elusive. These unidentified hunters were able to stock their larder for many weeks with their kill. Photographer, Silas Melander.

What was not immediately eaten was preserved for the long winter months in mason jars. Before the glass lid was placed on the jar, melted paraffin was poured over the preserves to insure an airtight seal (1890). Photographer, Horace Stevenson.

We are indebted to the photographers who were perceptive enough to record commonplace but vital characteristics of western life in the nineteenth century, for it was never easy to photograph people in the nineteenth century. They used the term "instantaneous picture" to try to resolve the difficulties created by slow emulsions and slow lenses and unavailable sources of light, but the candid picture was a phenomenon of the twentieth century only. To see such candid views of people living out their lives is a technological miracle that we can only applaud today. We are not often given the opportunity to examine the way in which people lived on the western frontier, and this example is an extraordinarily vivid indication of the way people faced frontier life in those days. Above all, there is the remarkable picture (following page), which might have been taken today under studio conditions, of a child in all the quiet innocence of her life clutching with enormous possessiveness a hand-carved doll (painfully made by a father, a loving brother—who knows who made it—still bearing a trace, if one examines the photograph closely, of the knife and chisel marks on the bare wood). Everything of the West can be seen in this picture: a lack of sophistication, of the carved doll and the rag doll, of the child, a wide-eyed innocence, a firm determination. This monumentally significant photograph tells us everything about the people who populated the West.

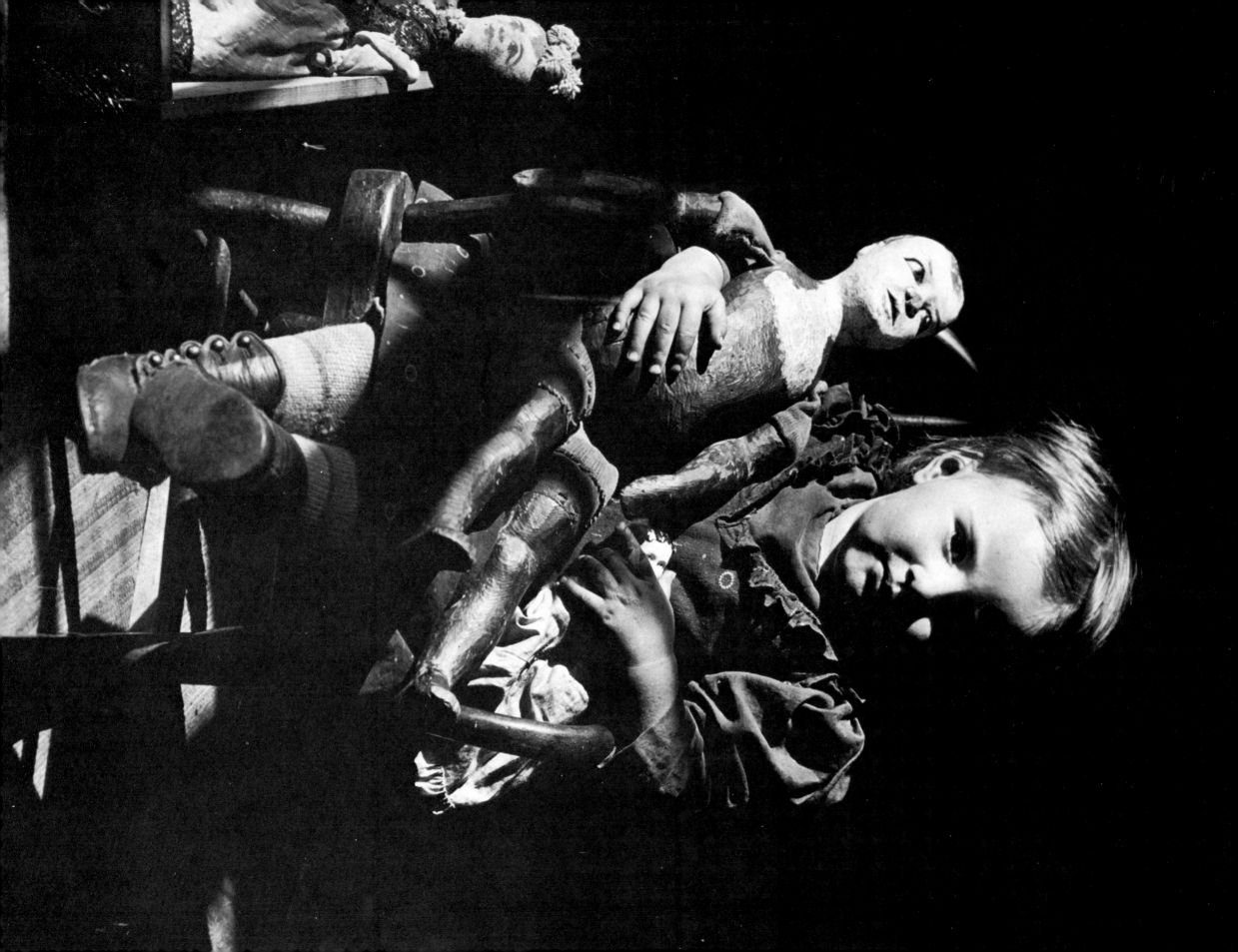

Here we see Silas Melander's intimate depiction of an early morning breakfast scene.

Opposite: Sitting with her wooden, rag, and china dolls, this lovely little girl waits patiently for photographer Silas Melander to take her picture. This photograph was taken in Deadwood, South Dakota, in the 1880s.

Such photographs of everyday home life are virtually unknown, for they date from a time when photography was posed, formal, rigid, and unyielding; it was difficult to make a photograph show the spirit, the feeling, the ambience, the excitement, the capriciousness of life itself. To see the interior of homes—badly lit, badly organized to provide adequate photographic opportunity—to catch people in the act of carrying through the requirements of day to day living, to glimpse the tender relationship implied here between the young children and the older men who act as guardians is a rare privilege; this photograph stands out in unaccustomed glory.

Opposite: In the 1880s, life in a small Deadwood, South Dakota, cabin was cramped, but many endured the hardships and stayed to look for gold. Photographer, Silas Melander.

A woman pores over an 1880s Montgomery Ward catalog. Photographer unknown.

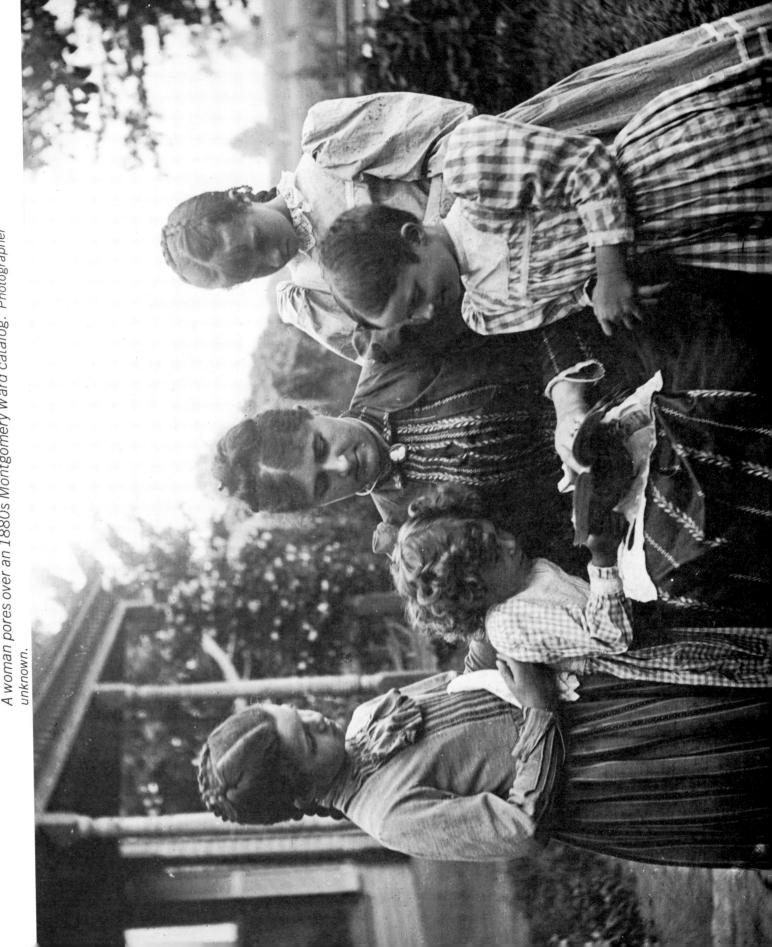

The suntanned, wrinkled faces bespeak of the care-worn life of this Harmon, Colorado, family in 1888. Photographer unknown.

The portrait of a family with their favorite mounted horse is not so uncommon, but it is indicative of much. Here is the beginning of the enclosure of the land by barbed wire. Here is a small community with a home nearby. But here, too, most important, is displayed the relationship of the older woman who is carefully tending the hand of the young child with his finger in his mouth. That enclosing hand, with the brilliant sharpness of the knuckle engraved through years of hard work, and the implacable expression of the woman who has faced every hazard of the frontier and survived it, together offer us a document that gives testimony to the kind of men and women that these photographs are full of, the kind of men and women who made the West.

A prairie farm family was visited by a barrage of traveling salesmen, always welcome with their exciting eastern wares. *Photographer, Silas Melander.*

We have made much of the loneliness of the West, especially before the railroad. But from earliest times the East came to the West because the West would not go to the East, though it had to ape the East's manners. Thus, early on, the classic Yankee peddler came West to exploit the new markets, new people, the new opportunities. Everything was sold everywhere a wagon could travel. Everything was demonstrated. To see this picture of a stove in use, demonstrating the advantages of the equipment to farming communities, is to speak of the ability of commerce to find its market in a building wilderness. (In this photograph it is interesting to notice the affliction of the old woman with her finger pressed into her ear to enable her to hear each of the silvered words of the salesman demonstrating the new stove, the new comforts, the new leisure, the harbingers of a new life that would eclipse the painful old life.)

The key to this building West, where it was available, was lumber. It was the durable material, the guarantee of permanence, of stability —except for fire. It was even a marketable product. The forests were green gold. No one ignored them. They were chopped down. The trees were sawed into planks. The wood was used on the spot—to build homes, to build barns, to build other mills—and every contrivance necessary to bring the wood to the mills was used. Tidewater was used where it was available. Dams were flung across creeks to control the flow of water so that the logs could be brought to the mill. Horses, oxen, sledges—everything was used to bring the logs to be sawed. No community that could make use of it ignored wood. Every Western community was built of wood—either in whole, or in part, until the new materials of stone and brick and mortar and cement could be substituted.

Lumbermen and sawmill operators were in great demand. Theirs were the kinds of skills that built the West; they were the kind of men who introduced into the West the Scandinavian spirit from the depleted forests of Minnesota and Wisconsin. The search for the lumber, the felling, the milling, the utilization, the building of bunkhouses and mess halls, the erection of lumber yards, the drying of lumber— all of the processes that went into the utilization of this most valuable material contributed much to the building West.

Here we have a collection of photographs that amply demonstrate, in all of its aspects, in all its varied characteristics, this extraordinary industry in the American West. Yet there is a curious anomaly in all of this. The original settlers, understanding their dependence on bountiful nature, were sufficiently awed by the cathedral-like grace of the redwood forest to let it stand, a tribute to its ability to touch their deepest natures. It was only later, much later, when reverence was replaced by greed, that the redwoods began to suffer. Despite his acute needs, the early settler had more sense and much more sensibility than his descendants.

To subdue the land the American prairie men needed lumber of every size, shape, and description. The construction of this Nebraska home was begun in 1892. Photographer, unknown.

Page 94: The forests of the north were cut in the winter months because it was easier to transport the heavy logs over the snow. Photographer, Silas Melander.

Page 95: Horses and mules dragged heavy-loaded sleds of logs to the riverbanks to stockpile for the spring float. Photographer, Silas Melander.

Lumber piled and ready for the downstream float, Minnesota, 1880s.
Photographer, Silas Melander.

Logs being rolled from the riverbank's stockpiles. Photographer, Silas Melander.

Opposite: The logs are landed and snaked up the riverbanks; then they are dragged into the sawmills. *Photographer, Silas Melander.*

Below: Once inside the mills, the logs, bark and all, are cut into boards. Both men in the foreground are leaning on a pick-like tool, used to pitch and roll the logs into position for the saw. *Photographer, Silas Melander.*

Opposite bottom: Stockpiled in the lumberyard were rough-cut pieces of wood, ready to be used for every kind of structure. *Photographer, Silas Melander.*

The hard-working lumberjacks enjoy a hearty meal in this cookhouse of the lumber camp. Photographer, Silas Melander.

Some trees withstood the onslaught of the loggers. This redwood, "Grizzly Giant," in Mariposa Grove, California, became a tourist attraction. Photographer, Silas Melander.

3 Hard-Rock Country

In coming to the West, the settlers came to the land and for the land. But they did not always know quite why they came. Frequently, they discovered the reason only after they arrived.

Those who came for the land in the main came to till it, to live upon it, to work on it, and to encourage it to yield that for which farmers and peasants have yearned for centuries. They wanted growing things —fruits, vegetables, trees—all the things that man could cut down, pull out, and use. Others came as fishermen come to the sea. They wanted to delve into the land, to get underneath the land. They wanted to extract those things within the land, its rich interior; they came for the silver, copper, iron, and above all, gold they *knew* were there.

There is a deep relationship between the search for gold in America and the impact of that search on the American character. The frenzy that gold aroused reflected itself in every kind of mining activity in every locality where it was suspected that King Midas's metal could be found. We know of placer mining, mining on the surface of the ground, and—a marvelously descriptive term—hardrock mining, which involved penetrating deep under the surface of the earth. What is not widely remembered is that the labor of gold recovery was backbreaking, endless, and killing. Only those who mined knew that the actual process of mining was for the young, that it was a lonely process, that it was an uncertain process, that while the investment of money to have others find gold might be profitable, the search for it frequently was not.

The advantages the miner experienced were rough, "outdoorsy," and, to the miner, of dubious value. While one could discover the magnificence of an unspoiled landscape in the quest for gold, one in fact had to endure immense privation, numbing cold, dreadful food, isolation from friends, forced habitation in the most bitter of circumstances; one had to become reconciled to the company of rough men, to rough play, to unpremeditated violence, and, ultimately, to difficult and hard death.

Such was the lot of hard-rock mining, placer mining, the fate of those who investigated the earth itself. Yet mining was commonplace in the West. It embraced at different times the lives and the fortunes of many men. It brought into play new skills, and it required the learning of old skills. It transformed men into moles, into ferrets, into underground laborers. It produced a strain of men whose strength and endurance are still unmatched. It created wealth. It created a myth. It created legends. It created millionaires.

The story of mining in the West is a story often told but rarely seen. Hence the value and significance of these photographs, for in them we have an opportunity to see a picture of a brief and meaningful stage in the development of the American character in the American West, one that has never been seen in photographs as brilliant as these.

Opposite: Most difficult of all was the hard-rock mining, here practiced by the men at the Kelly, New Mexico, mine, 1887. Photographer, Joseph E. Smith.

The Brown family on the Turnpike Road from Denver to Leadville, Colorado, 1880. The board strapped to the side of the wagon was used as a brake. It was placed in the spokes of the back wheels as the wagon was inched down the perilous mountain roads. Photographer unknown.

A characteristic of the mining life was the unpredictable demands it made on men and women for their attention and their work. The casual intermingling of the rough and the refined was ever present. It could not have been so unusual to see a miner dressed in shirtsleeves and a tie, with an overall coverall, pausing in the road with his family. We are fortunate that a photographer was on hand. Likewise, we are fortunate to have someone on hand to epitomize the commonplace Mexican miners in Socorro, New Mexico, bringing out of their hole in the ground the ore that they hoped would be refined and produce wealth, the dream of every miner. The primitive character of the tools—the top maul, the shovel—the frayed and tattered clothes, the piles of undistributed gravel and rock, the small boulders, the barren landscape, the dry and hot character of the scene, are all testimony to the wearying, graceless life that was the lot of those who tried to wrest riches from Mother Earth herself.

This early view near Yosemite Falls, California, in 1887, is indicative of the breathtaking scenery of the West. *Photographer, Silas Melander.*

Diverted, perhaps, by the natural beauty and glory of Yosemite, this miner turned hunter momentarily sits by his temporary lean-to with the carcass of a bear—the result of his skill—stretched out before him. His trophy is a monument to those who pitted themselves against the grandeur and the isolation of nature in the West.

Lonely settlers' cabin at the base of Yosemite Falls, 1877.
Photographer, Silas Melander.

Those who came first had the fortune to see the glories of the western scene in a way few have seen it since. Yosemite's falls, reflected in Mirror Lake, thunder in unspoiled magnificence, and the photographer bears eloquent testimony to man's ability to respond to the landscape's power.

There is a savage, bleak eloquence in this photo. Removed from mankind, with little evidence of his passing, isolated from all that makes living comfortable and meaningful, here is evidence of the solitary determination of a man or of men who begin a life in an unspoiled area. The sweep of the mountain foothills, the rising grandeur of the mountains etched against the sky, the somber darkness of the tall pines, the bitter character of the landscape, all suggest the endless labor and difficulty that had to be undergone to bring to this building site all of the material necessary to begin construction of a home, a place in which a new quest for fortune was being attempted by an unknown American.

This picture at right seems undistinguished: a group of small log buildings known in history as Gordon's Stockade, located on French Creek, near the present site of Custer City, South Dakota. But it is a silent monument to avidity and stupidity. It was here that a group known as the Gordon Party had penetrated the Black Hills in defiance of a treaty between the Indians of the area and the U. S. government,

a treaty that stated that the area was the Indian's alone, not to be invaded by white men for any reason whatever. Here they built a stockade to defend themselves against the outraged Indians. In their belief that the area was rich in gold, the miners were so relentless that they had to be forcibly removed by the U.S. Cavalry from Fort Laramie. The story typifies an episode that is redolent of avidity and greed, that stuff that flamed to violence and ended in death and bitter tragedy.

BLACK HILLS ART GALLERY.

114

Silas Melander's photographic gallery in the south bend of Deadwood Gulch, 1876. Mr. Melander is second from the left. Photo, Silas Melander Studio.

Opposite: Calamity Peak, South Dakota, 1876. Distinctive peaks often were given names and used as direction-finding guides. Photographer, Silas Melander.

South bend of Deadwood Gulch, 1876. Timberlines began to rise as Deadwood Gulch used more of the mountain lumber for construction. Photographer, Silas Melander.

In our time, we struggle against the mythical West. The myth is our legacy from the real West, but it is also the tragedy, for we do not know, nor can we adequately conceive of, the *real* West, the real towns, the real life. Here is an image of Deadwood Gulch, of the south bend of Deadwood Gulch —not in its rustic grandeur, but in all its primitive bleakness, its barrenness, its bitterness, its isolation. The fury of jerry-building for the sake of providing temporary housing for the ravishers of the earth, the miners of Deadwood Gulch, is its own indictment.

Deadwood Gulch. This is the Deadwood Gulch in which Wild Bill Hickok walked. This is the scene of a fury of speculative labor. This is the contribution, in all its mindless madness, that the miner, the settler, the gold-mine investor brought to the Black Hills, to the unsettled, primitive West. This is the contribution of progress.

There is nothing in Deadwood Gulch to relieve the gray and barren bitterness of this commercial enterprise. No planting of flowers. Nothing to relieve the plainness, the drabness, the instant utilization. Gravel is piled everywhere; wood is piled for use as shoring in the mines. No paint is used; no penny is spent to give beauty or a sense of pleasure and excitement to those who live here. Deadwood Gulch is pure, unadulterated, utilitarian town. Everything to show the disorderly character of human life can be observed here. The dress of the men, the random character of the tents, the sprawling use of logs everywhere, the unfinished roofs— all are witness to temporary expedience for the making of money, of impermanence.

Deadwood Gulch was a barren horror. And it is altogether fitting, perhaps a kind of blessing, that when Nature could no longer stand this drabness, she visited fire upon the town so at least the people could rebuild and be offered another chance to create a community in which men and women might live.

Main Street, Deadwood Gulch,
1876. Photographer, Silas Melander.

Deadwood, South Dakota, was officially established as a town in 1876. That same year photographer Silas Melander climbed the side of a mountain to get this exciting picture of Deadwood.

In this detailed close-up we see three Chinese laundries in one block.
Photographer, Silas Melander.

Looking closely, we can see that all the attributes of developing civilization are here in serried ranks: the National Hotel, a name repeated in every mining camp that dotted the West; the Cricket, a business of undetermined character; three Chinese laundrymen, each one competing to make the miners clean and presentable after their endless backbreaking labor; a tin shop, endlessly necessary in a primitive mining village. To look at this wooden village is to realize the necessity of a carpenter shop, and, of course, it is here. Every type of wheeled vehicle is here for repair, for rent, and for use—all of the elements to make it possible for this town, hewn out of the forest, to survive its streets—no five-foot length of which is without potholes. This is the reality of life, the real area, the real environment in which miners lived out their lives and found their satisfaction.

The bleakness goes on: the slashed hills—immense trees were cut down to provide the building lumber for the town below; the unplanned, chaotic development of the town—askew, a jumble; the tailing of the mine; the unrelieved, unwashed gravel. All of the impedimenta of a town that rushed on to temporary financial success, leaving strewn in its wake the refuse of an inconsiderate and an uncomprehending following. In the summer it is unbearable. In the winter, equally so. The hills at least are covered with the temporary blessing of the white snow, but the cold is freezing, numbing. Building is suspended because the wood is frozen and cannot be moved. It is a cold in which fires must be kept lit all day to provide the minimum of warmth to sustain life. The danger of fire—too often a danger realized—was constant in this town. One can only try to imagine the horror of winter days piled upon winter days in this isolated portion of the western wilderness: that was the reality of the West.

Opposite: Central City, Deadwood Gulch, 1876. Photographer, Silas Melander.

One can only imagine the bitter cold that hard-rock miners endured as they waited out the winters. Deadwood, 1876. Photographer, Silas Melander.

Gayville, South Dakota, 1876. Each miner used every scrap of material he could find to build shelter in the growing town. Photographer, Silas Melander.

Wood structures invited fires, which often devastated entire towns. In 1876, flames wiped out half of the town of Gayville, South Dakota. Photographer, Silas Melander.

Montana City, South Dakota, 1876, one of the many mining towns that sprung up in the Black Hills near Deadwood. Photographer, Silas Melander.

There was some pleasure in other mining communities, such as those farther up the foothills. At least in the summer there was the glory of the tall trees and their rich greenness, the invigorating, refreshing aspect of Nature to relieve man's handiwork. Yet, over all, the mining towns were all alike—groceries, saloons, restaurants, and wooden frame houses. This was life. Holes and ditches were dug where they were necessary, with a casual disregard for the amenities of life. Life took second place to need. Need was really a euphemism for greed.

Placer Claim, Blacktail Gulch, South Dakota, 1876. Ore shoveled in the wooden flume was washed by water from a nearby creek or spring. The gold metal would sink and settle behind baffles built into the wood flume, and the mud and lighter material would be washed away. Photographer, Silas Melander.

This was the true character of the hard-rock mining community of the West of its day; placer mining, the shoveling of endless tons of what is believed to be gold-bearing gravel into long, wooden troughs irrigated by running water in the hope that the gold will be filtered out, presented no more encouraging an aspect. The immensity of the labor is hard to calculate. The necessity to dispose of the water and of the non-gold-bearing gravel posed a problem too great for the miners to deal with, so they often left their "work" where it lay. The despoilment and indifference to the environment were beyond belief, though of course such matters were not even discussed in those halcyon days.

Placer Claim #1, Blacktail Gulch, 1876. Photographer, Silas Melander.

Water was the life-blood of the operation, and it was brought from everywhere. No form of transport was considered too difficult. Thus flumes, twisting their way through the mountains, down from the heights, where melting snows in the summertime were always available, were a common sight. Anything that was needed to bring water was done; and the skill of building flumes developed to a high art, as witness the elaborate system of trestles that made it possible to bring the water from where it originated to where it was needed. One must marvel at the great ingenuity expressed in the utilization of raw materials in the building of the flumes; but one must also wonder at the cost, to man and his surroundings.

Water flume on Whitewood Creek, Black Hills, 1876. Water was at a premium. Flumes like this went for miles to the gold placer diggings. Photographer, Silas Melander.

A section of the Spring Creek water flume passed by the Dunlaps Ranch in the Black Hills, 1876. Photographer, Silas Melander.

138

Finally, we come to one of the most ancient and most onerous of man's activities—burrowing in the ground for the rich minerals stored within. The date at which these pictures were taken makes the clarity of the photographs unexpected, but even so we cannot see photographs of miners at work. The noise, the dust, the confusion, and the flickering light that attended the labor made interior photography impossible. Thus we have the photographer and his assistants coming down to photograph the mine as it stood. But from the outside it is not too difficult to conceive of the inside. And nowhere have we ever seen pictures better illustrating the mine than we see in these photographs, taken underground.

Down in a mine at Kelly, New Mexico, 1887, photographer Joseph E. Smith needed three assistants to light the dark mine with flash powder.

Kelly, New Mexico, 1887. In the well-composed picture you can almost feel the overbearing weight on the shored-up mine shaft. Photographer, Joseph E. Smith.

Gold, lead, and zinc yielded to the pick in the mines at Kelly, New Mexico, 1887. Streaks of the ore can be seen in the ceilings. Photographer, Joseph E. Smith.

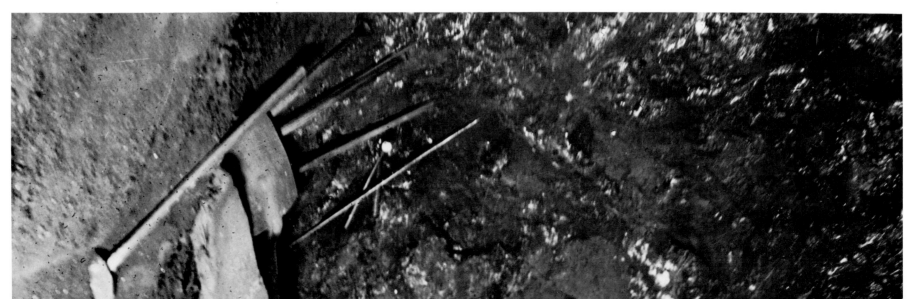

Assay laboratory in the School of Mines, Socorro, 1886. Photographer, Joseph E. Smith.

There is almost a contrived innocence in the delicate relationship of the materials that go to make up this scene of an assay office—the heart and the center of the gold mining system. This was where the miner found out whether his sample was gold. Men's fortunes literally hung on the words of the assayist. This was the point of no return, the moment of truth in which all the labor and all the investment was realized or not.

Above: The Black Hills Smelting Works, 1876. Employees worked night and day to keep up with the ore that needed to be refined. Photographer, Silas Melander.

Opposite top: Billings Smelter, Socorro, 1887. Lead and zinc pigs are molded and shipped east to waiting paint manufacturers. Photographer, Joseph E. Smith.

Opposite bottom: Billings Smelter, Socorro, 1887. Cars of molten metal are shunted to various areas of the smelter, where the metal is processed and molded into pig bars. Photographer, Joseph E. Smith.

At every mine there was the smelter, a huge cauldron of boiling metal in which the gold and the impurities were separated. The smelter needed only heat and skilled labor. It required no refinements of building, no decoration. Here we see it in all of its utilitarian splendor, functioning, providing the answer, long-sought by everyone who toiled in the earth. To those who worked at the smelter it had little meaning. They were merely laborers, frequently skilled, but poorly paid, but they held the key to other men's fortunes.

In these pictures (opposite), taken in natural light—a technical tour de force—one can see the spilling of the molten liquid into "pigs" so that they can be transported and sold on the world metal market. The whole system is made manifest in the labor—the dirty, grueling, sweltering, brutish labor—that transformed work into other men's wealth.

4 The Dispossessed

Presently, when interest in the American Indian has quickened, it is popular and easy to think of a hundred and fifty years of relations between Indians and non-Indians as a single problem—as, in short, *the* Indian problem. Such a treatment makes for easy consideration—and easy dismissal. But there is a more profound truth: the many aspects of a farflung and diverse problem. There were many Indian problems, none of them easy to solve, few properly documented.

Unfortunately, it was not until the 1900s that Indians accepted the camera with relative ease and the state of the art developed to the point that photographs of the reality of Indian tribal life could be taken. Many photographs taken of Indians in the 1870s have proved to be of immense ethnological and anthropological value, but the vigor and intensity of the conflict between the Indians and the armies of the United States rendered impracticable and virtually impossible the opportunity to photograph the more pressing and meaningful realities of Indian life.

Thus, unhappily, the largest body of photographs of Indians that we have are those that were taken in the 1890s and after, when the Indian had been subjugated. Thus we are witness, all too frequently, to photographs of a defeated people—humiliated, discouraged, hopeless. The carnival Indian, the sideshow Indian, became a symbol of the period. Indians dressed in combinations of costumes that had nothing to do with the rich quality of a tradition that had nourished many proud people, had helped them endure privation, agony, betrayal, and defeat. These traditions were no longer represented. Moreover, in order to provide reassurance, every effort was made to present the Indians as a people no longer able to defend their birthright, their future, their land, their lives. All too often photographs showed people who had passed from subjugation to resentment, to indifference, to total apathy.

In spite of this, there is strong photographic evidence of a people still vigorous in their memories of ancient pride, still proud in their recollections of victories won and lives honorably spent. There are Indians of proud lineage, Crows, Piegans, Salish. These were men and women who still could recall that a scant forty or fifty years earlier their warriors had been justly feared, that their tribes had been able to defend themselves against the encroaching whites, that they had represented a source of terror to the settlers, their armies, and their government representatives.

This Indian, the celebrated Crow Plenty Coups, was a warrior of notable reputation, a man honored not only by his people but by those who considered him an enemy, a man whose life was devoted to the traditional ways, whose knowledge encompassed wisdom and respect for the great spirits, who knew his relation to the earth and honored it with his care and with his reverence. For him the flag in his hand was a flag he wished to embrace although the way was hard. He was a man who failed in his efforts to reconcile his people with a government that was never able to explain itself satisfactorily. He stands a symbol of a conflict that was never satisfactorily resolved, one that remains on both the national conscience and the national agenda of the United States of America.

Preceding page: The great Chief Plenty Coups of the Crow tribe in northern Montana, 1908. Plenty Coups's father trained his five-year-old son for running by telling him that if he caught a butterfly, he would be like the butterfly: quick and graceful. Plenty Coups related the story to his friends, and soon all the little Indian boys were chasing butterflies all over the camp. *Photographer, N. A. Forsyth.*

Left to right: Buffalo Bill, Prince Albert of Monaco, and Chief Plenty Coups. The pictures were taken on the main street of Cody, Wyoming, 1913. Buffalo Bill is introducing Prince Albert to Chief Plenty Coups. Upon handing Chief Plenty Coups his gift of a rifle, Prince Albert was quoted to say, "I trust you will only hunt with this rifle and not use it against the white man."

Nez Perce Indians on a reservation in western Montana, 1908. The canvas teepee was issued by the reservation Indian agents. Photographer, N. A. Forsyth.

Salish Indians on a reservation in northwestern Montana, 1908.
Photographer, N. A. Forsyth.

Reenactment of the battle scene at Big Horn Valley, in which the Indians defeated General George Armstrong Custer's Seventh Cavalry. Photographer unknown.

For many years Curley, Crow scout for Custer and survivor of the Battle of Big Horn, was plagued to tell his version of the battle at the Greasy Grass. Photographer, N. A. Forsyth.

Both kinds of Indians, the defeated and the proud, are represented in these photographs of the native American.

This is an Indian sitting on his pony, solid, truculent, determined, an Indian of some fame, Curley, a Crow—a man who, in his youth, was employed by the Seventh Cavalry as a scout and was, perhaps, the only living survivor, among the Indians, of the annihilation of that force at the battle of Little Big Horn. This is a man who spent his years puzzled, annoyed, harassed, resentful of the interminable questioning to force him to restate his views, or even to rethink them with respect to the passions that flared on both sides of this ill-fated military venture. Wearing a buffalo robe, he sits on his pony, a symbol of the Indian's refusal to make sense of the ideological and intellectual conflicts between white men and Indians, a massive and powerful symbol of the Indian-white confrontation.

Chief Charlot of the Salish tribe with his family in western Montana,
1908. *Photographer, N. A. Forsyth.*

Salish squaws pose unwillingly for a portrait in western Montana, 1907. Photographer, N. A. Forsyth.

Wild Gun and his squaw pose for pictures in front of their beautifully decorated teepee in northern Montana, 1907.
Photographer, N. A. Forsyth.

There is much to be seen in examining these photographs. Although this teepee is canvas, army regulation duck, the ancient and honored tradition of painting the teepee to record Indian history and tribal relations persists. The clothes and the bearings of these men and women indicate a continuing concern and respect for the maintenance of the old ceremonials on which the richness and spirituality of Indian life depended.

Little Dog, chief of the Piegan Indians, and squaw pose in a rare interior view of a teepee, 1910. Photographer, N. A. Forsyth.

Page 164: Piegan Indian, northern Montana.

Page 165: Chief Louison of the Salish Indians, 1908.

Bear Chief, a Piegan, posing with his favorite pony in western Montana, 1910. Photographer, N. A. Forsyth.

Some men at any time in their lives embody a continued tradition, a posture, an attitude, a vigorous feeling for life that cannot be denied. This Indian, standing as he does, looking into the camera with the confidence of a man sure of himself, willing to accept the social structure of which he is a part, is a key reminder of the kind of attitude that led so many early settlers to speak of the Indians as "hostiles," failing to comprehend that they faced only men as determined as they themselves were—on the one side, to find a new life in a land of their choosing, and, on the other, to defend their homeland to the death.

Opposite: Piegans preparing for Sun Dance in the Medicine Lodge, 1910. In the foreground are crackers and other foods issued to the Indians by the reservation agents. Photographer, N. A. Forsyth.

Salish Indians smoking the pipe of peace in western Montana, 1908. Photographer, N. A. Forsyth.

Of particular interest is the curious lack of response and empathy between the photographer and the Indian subjects—in all cases, from young to old on the part of the Indians there is a puzzling, questioning noninvolvement, as though the taking of a photograph is a duty to be borne. The subjects of the photographs reject the honor and pleasure that any Indian would feel under different circumstances.

Piegan maidens wait for the Choosing Dance to begin. Northern Montana, 1907. Photographer, N. A. Forsyth.

Wood Chief Woman praying at the Sun Dance in western Montana, 1910. Tribes came from reservations all over the Northwest to attend these ceremonies. Photographer, N. A. Forsyth.

Unwitting but obvious social tragedy is shown in this picture of Indians surrounded by an admiring white audience, expecting to see the Indians display for them the most sacred of their religious ceremonies—an audience uncomprehending, unappreciative, and, in the end, derisive. It is appalling to think that a people would be asked to display their deepest religious feelings for the diversion and pleasure of the bored.

Roast dog was a common meal for the Cree tribe. Western Montana, 1908. Photographer, N. A. Forsyth.

Page 176: Chief Moise of the Salish tribe poses with his family on a reservation in northern Montana, 1908. Photographer, N. A. Forsyth.

Page 177: The Piegan Choosing Dance, northern Montana, 1908. Photographer, N. A. Forsyth.

There is much to study in the depictions of these fine Piegan warriors. Every detail of each handcrafted ornament had great significance for the Indian. Photographer, N. A. Forsyth.

These five Piegan warriors offer a picture of bleak tragedy. Living days that have, for them, little meaning, dressed in the vestiges of the clothes of days that had great meaning, faced with the contradiction of a time they can neither understand nor master, trying to live as old men recalling days that have passed them by forever, failing to find the necessary sustenance and comfort in memories, however glorious, that would make the present an endurable moment, they simply exist.

Piegan Chief All Over and his family in northern Montana, 1909.
Photographer, N. A. Forsyth.

Enlarged detail shows All Over's papoose at the opening of the tee-pee. *Photographer, N. A. Forsyth.*

Champion wrestler of the Salish Indians, 1907. Photographer, N. A. Forsyth.

Opposite: A Salish family in western Montana poses for pictures on a western Montana reservation, 1907. Photographer, N. A. Forsyth.

Julius Meyer's Indian Wigwam Store, Omaha, Nebraska, c. 1875. Mr. Meyer, an Indian interpreter, accompanied the Indians on their many treaty-signing trips to Washington. Photographer unknown.

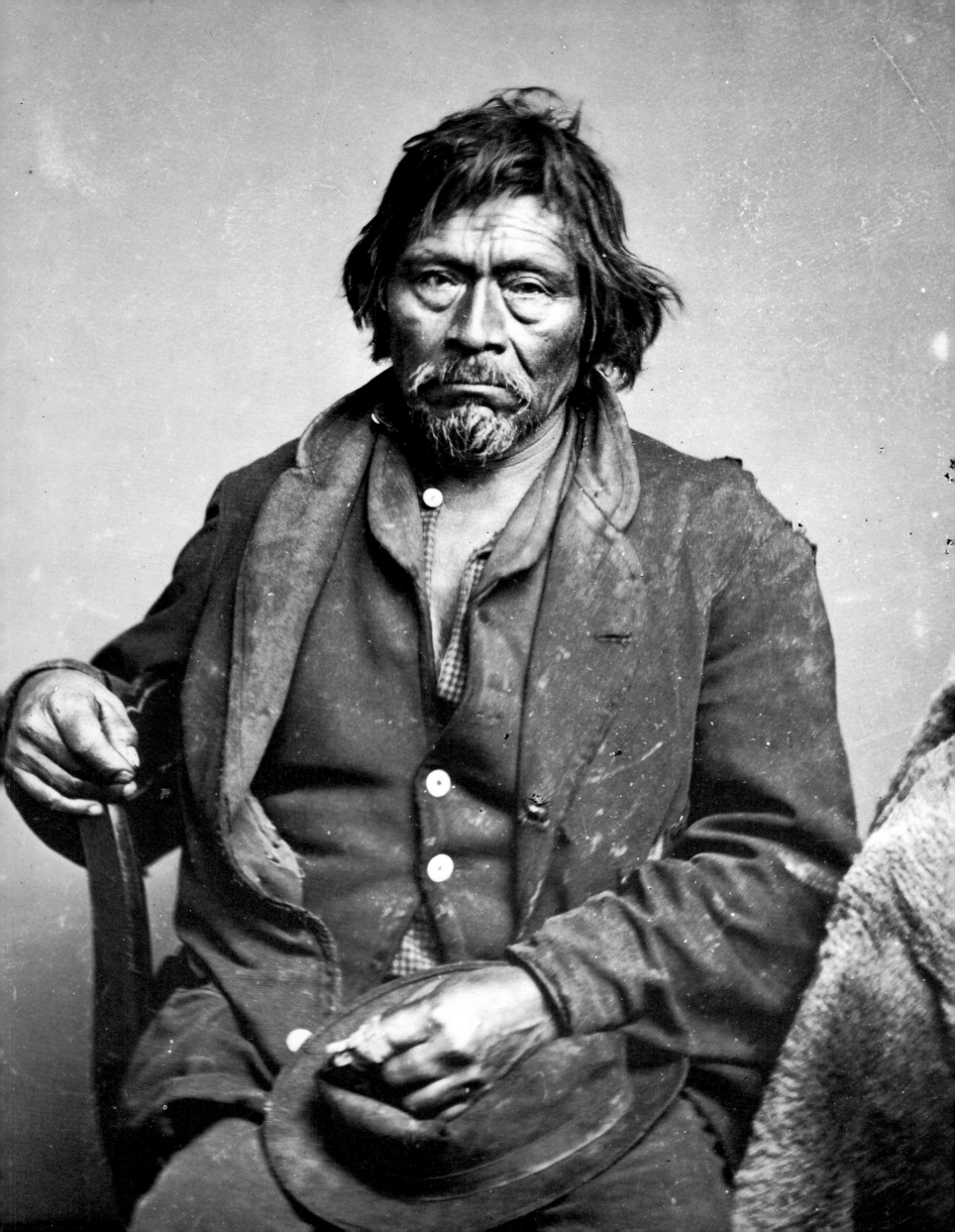

Opposite: On his 1877 trip to the West, Silas Melander photographed this Paiute medicine man.

Comanches of Quanah Parker's band, Cache, Oklahoma, 1910.
Photographer unknown.

Comanche women of Quanah Parker's band, Oklahoma, 1910. Photographer unknown.

More than two hundred Shebits were baptized by the Mormons at St. George, Utah. Photographer unknown.

The lodge is raised for the Sun Dance on a western Montana Indian reservation, 1912.
Photographer, N. A. Forsyth.

The richness of Indian life comes through in the picture of the raising of a Piegan lodge by all the grown and able men in the community. Blessed by the Indian in ceremonial costume, who stood as a symbol of the supremacy of man over his environment, at the same time they are celebrating with the Sun Dance the relationship of a man who is submissive to his environment, respecting it and using it with discretion, taste, understanding, and a deep and abiding love.

The drama in this picture suggests the often remarked-upon eloquence of Indian oratory. The astonishing vigor and the penetrating ability of the Indians to express themselves in natural imagery—eloquent, moving, tender, and sharply focused—is a memorable legacy to the literature of the United States. Spoken in a tongue few could master, the expressiveness and richness of gesture that accompanied the speeches mark the Indians as a people who spoke out of a love for the earth on which their souls and spiritual life were based.

5 The Land Subdued

The settlers came to know that the land in its many aspects was both their friend and enemy. They came to know that they needed the support of the land, and they wooed it—tenderly, lovingly, and, above all, faithfully. And they were rewarded. They also learned that the land needed to be fought, and it was fought and, in time, subdued. The taming of the land was done with grace, with vigor, with passion, with love, with devotion, with ferocity, with endurance; but it was *done*.

These pictures give us an indication of the transformation of the windswept prairies where the wind blew clean, of the small adobe-and-buffalo-chip hovels. The shacks were replaced with houses of size and substance. The wild cattle were tamed so that herds could be driven to slaughter and sold to a people who had learned not only to eat meat but to demand it as a normal part of their diet, who had invented machinery to replace the endless labor of men, who had developed machines to replace the horses, who had developed new methods for raising foods in quantity. The devotion to labor, the single-mindedness of effort that characterized their forebears, was at an end forever; one could dream of success in different terms—the land, the ever-present, bountiful, capricious, difficult land, had been conquered. A new time had opened for the descendants of the Americans who went west.

The message of this photograph, a witness to the contribution of the machine, is expressed most simply in the fact that forty years previously this young boy, playing so gently and lovingly with his dog, would have been an overworked youngster, tirelessly tramping back and forth across the field to lend his meager manpower to help the farmer in his never-ending struggle.

Kansas wheat field, 1904. Photographer, Harry Putney.

Family on their Nebraska ranch, c. 1900. As the years went by, this family prospered. More horses, more land, and more equipment bespoke of their tireless enterprise. Photographer unknown.

The spirit did change. With great precision the windmill is marked "Enterprise." How fitting a comment to mark the transformation of hard labor into enterprise! How pointed to notice that the land, the product of man's labor, was in the process of being changed by man's inventiveness, his ingenuity! Enterprise—the ability to use other forces—was a harbinger of the fact that the land itself no longer could refuse to yield its bounty to those who could bring the machines to their aid.

You can almost smell the pinewood siding on this Nebraska farmhouse, 1898. The well has been dug, the crops planted, and the preserves stored in the fruit cellar. Finally, there was time to make the children a wagon and a swing. Photographer unknown.

And now there is leisure. A direct consequence of the successful struggle against the land, it was the prized ingredient that was unimagined by those who preceded us; leisure, time for play, recognition that it is proper and fitting that children should play instead of work. A little wagon stands against the house. The people pause to be photographed in the course of a work day, to demonstrate with pride their new home and, most of all, the notion that the outlines of the good life—of leisure, of the ability and the means to play—are at last at hand. For many immigrant farmers, dreams spawned in feudal tyranny, nurtured in class bondage, had become realities on America's western plains.

Wyoming ranch scene, c. 1895. Whining through the air, the lariat finds its mark, and a steer is singled out of the herd. Photographer, Silas Melander.

Every era and every transformation has its symbols. In the West the water barrel was one, the wagon wheel another. Yet another was the sigh and swish of the swung lariat. The cowboy, here caught in malicious, exquisite motion, hurls his lariat with precision. The cattle mill about, waiting to be herded into their night's resting place. The lonely prairie, the low, sloping barn, are etched in sharp relief against the evening sky. The impact of the great cattle drives, of the cattle industry that grew out of it, of the towns that supported the industry, of the men who came to work in it, cannot be overemphasized in a discussion of the West; cattle were a massive force of change in the western plains of the United States in the nineteenth century.

The literature of the West, the music of the West, the sight and sound of the West—these are made up of the sounds of the lowing of cattle, the bawling of great herds moving across the plains from north to south, shepherded by cowboys—taciturn, morose men who did the work of the world. The area was studded with ranches, the whole surrounded by legends, myths, epics on which Americans have established their ideals and their traditions. And the camera has once again performed its vital function of offering us believable, vivid images of a time, of an event, of a feeling in history, a living, rich tapestry of our past. It is nearly impossible in cities, traveling on the freeways, flying over the land, to realize that not long ago the country, at least the western part of it, was made largely of desert areas, huge rocky mountains, and fantastic carpets of trees.

Oklahoma cattle ranch, 1910. Signs of prosperity were beginning to dot the countryside, and ranches like this became a more frequent sight in the West. Photographer unknown.

Clearing land meant cutting down trees and pulling the stumps. The stumps were massive, deeply rooted; centuries of growth underlay the spreading roots. It required more than sheer labor could bring to bear, and in the end, ingenuity, hard-won and cleverly fashioned, provided the means. Here, when the gear, the means, and the techniques are all but forgotten, the camera offers us a chance to share in the vigorous labor of pulling stumps.

Homestead in Nebraska, 1900. One of the most difficult tasks involved in clearing the land for farming was pulling out the stumps. Photographer, Silas Melander.

They called them hayburners: horses, the moving agent before the automobile. Most of the labor too heavy for men to do was undertaken by these willing animals. Day and night, they were harnessed and unharnessed to go forth to do the immense labor of the plains. No task was too onerous, no work too difficult, no sacrifice so great that it could not be asked of the horse, in many ways the greatest friend of the plains farmer.

Bakersfield, California, 1900. Land development occurred so quickly that street signs often were fixed before the streets were actually plowed. *Photographer unknown.*

Idaho farm, c. 1898. Teams of men and horses planted seed and cultivated the farmland. *Photographer, Silas Melander.*

*Night harvesting in Nebraska, early 1900s. The
land yielded bumper crops, and harvesting continued well into the night.*
Photo, Melander Brothers Studio.

Some have likened machines to beasts, and one wonders why. It is only under certain circumstances that the monstrous, straining efficiency and the awkward strange power of beasts are represented by machines in action. And it is on the prairie, where machines of huge size were needed to perform tremendous tasks, that every so often the camera would see what man could not see and offer it for his vision. Such a picture of machines is here presented as we witness the endless labor of making the prairie into the granary of the country.

Wheat harvesting on the Nebraska prairie, early 1900s. Photo, Melander Brothers Studio.

Once started, the process could not be reversed. There could never be enough machines, never a good enough machine. There could only be more machines and better machines. The farmers knew that this was so and supported every advance. There was no device that was not given a trial, and these devices in themselves and with man's help were the transforming agents of a growing, agricultural West. The machines did their work; they were efficient and profitable; they answered the need. But like all machines, they required their attendants, their servants, their admirers, their lovers, and all these were found. They were of all ages and all experiences. They looked different, one from another, and they acted that way. They came from every

corner of the world and from every obscure corner of the country. The cooks, the servants, the oilers, the engineers, the loaders, the stackers, the drivers, the teamsters, the old and the young, the black and the white, the educated and the ignorant—all came to tend the machines and to serve them, and in so doing they served the cause the machines themselves served. As time passed, machines and men were welded into a major effort to make it possible for the nation to conquer its deserts and its plains and to transform them into fruitful abundance for its people.

Kiowa, Kansas, wheat field at harvest time, c. 1915. Photographer, That Man Stone.

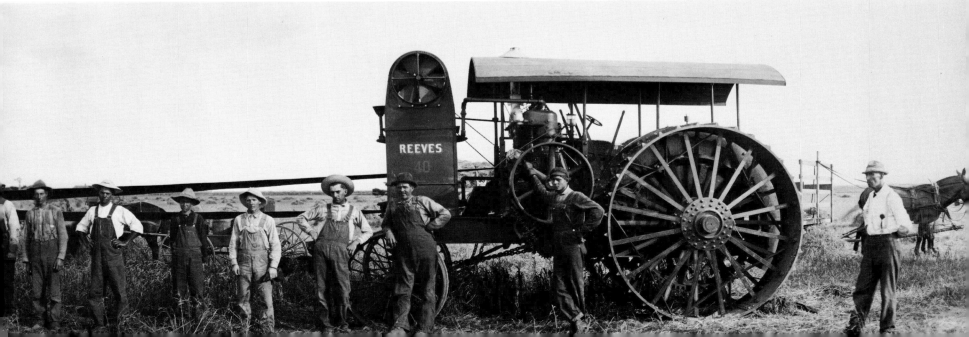

Prairie farmers at harvest, early 1900s. Photo, Melander Brothers Studio.

This cookhouse on wheels followed the harvesters from field to field.
Nebraska, early 1900s. Photo, Melander Brothers Studio.

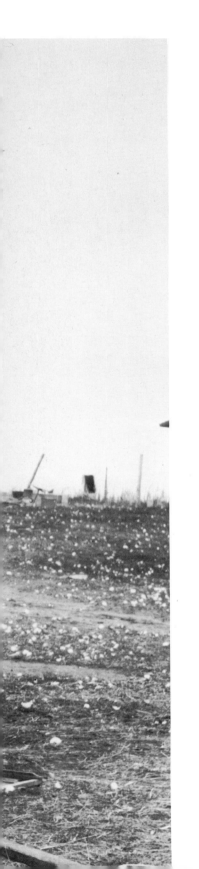

Grain from the plains was shipped east to mills. Pictured is a mill in Illinois. Photographer, Silas Melander.

To keep up with the agricultural boom, salesmen
brought their wares to the ranchhouse door. Iowa,
1900s. *Photographer, Silas Melander.*

Following page: Northern California, 1905. Much of the work was done, and there was time for picnics. Photographer unknown.

The subduing of the land was a struggle, a fight. But as in all such struggles, the violence came to an end, and with its passing came the knowledge and satisfaction of a worthy battle won and, not the least of its fruits, a new leisure, a new ability to stand back, to survey, to admire, to enjoy. This development manifested itself in picnics, cake-baking, swimming in rivers, horseback riding, building towns, and much else. It created a cultural basis that was part of the changing process in this country.

Isolated communities could no longer bear the burdens of the immense transformations already in the wind. Towns and cities were needed. Communication was needed. The parts had to become a whole. And so the land that was fallow or that could be used for cities was promoted, sold, built upon; slowly, that which had been the isolated prairie where the wind blew clean began to take the look of a prairie dotted with budding cities and busy people.

St. Joseph, Missouri, 1930s. A nation on wheels is fostered by the new industrial age and mass-production. Photographer, Edward Prawitz.

The Midwest was beginning to find its place as a link between the industrious seaboards, East and West. The word "success" began to appear more often in the speech and thinking of America. It was possible to see an abundance, almost an excess, of what it took to live. It was possible for all to believe and dream new dreams. Great things were happening. Greater things were promised. This was the heady tonic that pervaded the air in America as a consequence of the struggle to find the land, to come to it, to struggle with it, to subdue it, and to build upon it. Man began to transport himself, not on his feet, not on the back of an animal, but in a motorcar.

Leavenworth, Kansas, early 1900s. The streets are paved, and the automobile begins to replace the horse. Photographer, Horace Stevenson.

The gasoline engine became a success. Pneumatic tires were a realized possibility. Regarded skeptically, even cynically, the pre-eminence of cars soon was assured and the nation moved with easy self-confidence into a time when the main streets needed to be paved. Horses became something to be talked about and remembered with nostalgia, and the view of the city lined with hitching rails became a view of a city designed with parking areas and lines of cars, early cars, Jitneys; the Fords, the Chevrolets, the Dodges, all of these became the new literature, the new watchword, the standby, the new visual image, the new America.

Dillon, Montana, c. 1900. At last the land was subdued. Horatio Alger's dream began to come true. Photographer unknown.

Index

Note: Boldface numbers indicate material that appears in photos or captions.

Technical Appendix

Good photographic print quality with excellent overall image definition and optimum tone range, black to white, can be obtained from original early positive or negative material. The restoration of the original daguerreotype, tintype, or glass or nitrate film negative involves problems unique to each item and therefore cannot be discussed in general terms. But once the negative has been prepared, and barring special problems—which unfortunately are common—I have been able to make good prints from seemingly unprintable glass negatives and daguerreotypes by maintaining close control of negative density readings with a transmission densitometer and by using different equipment, light sources, chemistry, and lenses.

Although the printing treatment for each original glass negative is different, good results usually may be achieved with the following equipment, materials, methods, and procedures.

• ENLARGERS

Print contrast and image sharpness can be raised or lowered according to the negative by using an enlarger with a cold light source for low contrast and a point light source with condensers for high contrast and sharp image.

Caesar Saltzman enlarger 8 x 10 converted to 11 x 14 negative accommodation. Point light source. Mercury vapor. Condenser system with point light and 500-watt enlarging bulb #302. Aristo Grid light.

Omega D-2 enlarger 4 x 5, with point light source and condensers. Enlarging bulb #212 with variable condenser system.

5 x 7 E-3 Omega enlarger with cold light source.

5 x 7 Durst 138S enlarger with point light source and Aristo Grid cold light.

• ENLARGING LENSES

Schneider Componon	2X Plan Achromat Nikon
Nikon El Nikkor	3X Plan Achromat Nikon
Nikon Macro Nikkor	4X Plan Achromat Nikon
Rodenstock Rodagon	10X Plan Achromat Nikon
1.2 Plan Achromat Nikon	C.P. Goerz Apochromat Artars

• PHOTOMICROGRAPHIC SYSTEMS (used on a vibration eliminator base)

Nikon Multiphot   Nikon Microflex Model AFM used on a Nikon Microscope

• ILLUMINATION & FILTERING

For transmission negative enlarging: collimated light; Kohler illumination, central, oblique, and dark field illumination.

To copy with Panchromatic film, place a #58 Eastman green filter in the light path.

To copy daguerreotypes and tintypes, place polarization filters over the copy lights and the camera lens to vary the degree of reflection and shadow detail.

• PHOTOGRAPHIC PRINTING PAPERS AND FILMS

Eastman Poly Contrast Rapid Enlarging paper	Eastman Commercial film #6127
AGFA Brovira photographic enlarging paper	Eastman Contrast Process Ortho film #4154
Eastman Professional Copy film #4.25	Eastman Masking film
Eastman Super XX Pan film #4142	

• CONTACT PRINTING AND PAPER

Morse Contact printer with argon light source

Eastman AZO contact printing paper

Contact prints are also made under the enlarger with enlarging paper

• FILM DEVELOPER

Eastman HC110, Eastman D-19, Eastman DK-50, Eastman D-11, Eastman DK-60, Eastman D-76, Eastman D-23, Windisch.

• PAPER DEVELOPER & HYPO

Eastman Dektol diluted 2 water 1 developer stock solution

Eastman Dektol diluted 3 water 1 developer stock solution

Eastman Dektol diluted 6 water 1 developer stock solution

Eastman Selectol and Selectol Soft with Dektol as second developer

Eastman Rapid Fix Hypo bath

• BLEACHING

To bleach: use a solution of 10-20 grains of potassium ferricyanide in 8 ounces of water and apply to the print with a cotton swab; then the print is dipped in a hypo bath, with a contrast tone reduction. Test the bleaching on a discarded print for strength of bleach.

To bleach without losing contrast: use 10-20 grains of ammonium persulphate in 1 ounce of water. Apply to the local area of the print with cotton.